The Heartbreak of Conversation

and
Why Men Should Never Wear Pretty Stockings

NATHAN GRAHAM

iUniverse, Inc.
Bloomington

The Heartbreak of Conversation
And Why Men Should Never Wear Pretty Stockings

iUniverse books may be ordered through booksellers or by contacting:

iUniverse
1663 Liberty Drive
Bloomington, IN 47403
www.iuniverse.com
1-800-Authors (1-800-288-4677)

ISBN: 978-1-4759-5401-2 (sc)
ISBN: 978-1-4759-5400-5 (hc)
ISBN: 978-1-4759-5399-2 (e)

Library of Congress Control Number: 2012918483

Printed in the United States of America

iUniverse rev. date: 10/10/2012

Introduction

● ● ● ● ● ● ● ● ● ● ● ● ● ● ● ● ● ● ● ●

EVEN AS A SMALL child, I remember being convinced that I would one day lead a life of independence, acclaim and a complete lack of hives. Unfortunately for me, I have found very little independence, no acclaim and hives in some extremely sensitive areas of my body – at some of the most awkward moments imaginable. It's been difficult for me to pinpoint exactly where things began to go awry but through the years I have found myself surrounded by the kind of nasty, colorful characters that tend to inhibit independence, acclaim and a hive-free existence. When combined with my essentially thorough lack of focus, it's little wonder that my childhood goals have yet to be realized.

The night my only child was born was a memorable night on many levels. Like a trooper, I had witnessed a portion of the actual birth but was eventually forced to excuse myself before completion due to being severely grossed out. Dizzy and disconcerted, I took the elevator down to the hospital's lobby and made my way outside for a timely breath of fresh air. As I stood on the sidewalk gazing into the darkness of a warm June night, I became aware of some muted wheezing and hacking directly to my left. Glancing over, I spied a really decrepit looking fellow dressed in a baby blue robe and hooked up to some kind of portable contraption that provided concentrated oxygen. The elderly, barefoot man was passing continual gas and taking exaggerated drags on a cigarette that reeked of clove. An apparent rupture in the man's left cheek concerned me but his smoking concerned me even more.

"Hey, how ya doin'?" I asked cordially as I ambled over in his direction. He grunted something inaudible in response but I'm pretty sure I recognized the word "spavin".

"Nice night out. Bad night to be in there," I said, nodding back into the direction of the hospital building behind us. I paused for a few seconds and then, "So what are you in here for?"

The barefoot, stinking man took another long puff on his skinny little cigarette. "Me? I'm in here because I'm having complications with my emphysema --can't hardly breathe. Can't eat, can't piss. Quack says I'll be dead in a week. You know what? I don't care. I really don't. If I'm dead in a week, I'm dead in a week. It'll do me some good."

He must have seen something in the look on my face that amused him. The old man began laughing – a deep, hearty laugh – that soon dissolved into a fit of coughing and wheezing that, frankly, intimidated me. When it was over, he removed a wad of paper from the side pocket of his robe and wiped his mouth and nose with a trembling hand. He dropped the soiled paper to the sidewalk and pointed the same trembling hand in my direction.

"You ever hear of the Panic of 1837?" he asked me.

"Um, no…can't say that I have."

"Son, the Panic of 1837 was Van Buren's Waterloo. It came about because Van Buren was an arrogant son of a bitch. He mismanaged our country to the brink of extinction and then blamed the Whigs when he couldn't get another term."

"Really? I never knew any of that."

"And don't even get me started about Muriel Spark."

I didn't plan to. "So…do you think it's a good idea for you to be out here smoking in your condition?"

"If I'm not smoking, someone else will be."

"Well, sure," I continued deliberately, "but don't you think it makes things worse for you…for your condition? I mean -- if I was as sick as you are, the last thing I would be doing is smoking."

"Son, my smoking don't make no difference. It's just a pittance. You ever been to a bank?"

"Yes, of course."

"Well, there you go." The old man took another puff from his dwindling cylinder and painstakingly suppressed several more coughs.

The two of us stood there wordless for another half hour or so, watching just a wee bit of traffic navigating the road in front of the hospital. Abruptly, it occurred to me that I had completely forgotten about the birth of my child up on the fourth floor. I charged back into the lobby, eschewed the elevator and rushed up the stairs, reaching the fourth floor in mere seconds.

It was already pretty much over. My son had been completely born and was being handled professionally by a motherly nurse from the ward. As I peered through the glass into the nursery, I felt no disconnect whatsoever with my newborn son…none at all. He had more hair than I imagined he would but appeared otherwise nondescript and awfully well behaved.

I tiptoed into my wife's room, expecting an icy reception, but she was actually in very good spirits, obviously pleased to have the ordeal behind her. I began a tenuous explanation of where I had been but she simply waved me off and shook her head nonchalantly -- reclined, relaxed and comfortable in a bed for the first time in a long while. The doctor came in, however, and she wasn't nearly as forgiving.

"What's wrong with you? Do you have a screw loose?"

"No…I was just outside talking about the Panic of 1837 with a sick man who…"

"This was the birth of your first child! How could you miss it for any reason?"

"Well, I…"

"Come on! You're going with me!" The doctor grabbed me hard around the bicep and pulled me from my wife's room. She was a tiny oriental woman but was deceptively powerful. I attempted to resist but resistance seemed futile and the pain in my arm seemed anything but minor.

The doctor dragged me down a narrow hallway and into the elevator. She punched the number 7 and, taciturn, the two of us traveled to the hospital's highest floor. She never relaxed her grip on my arm and when the elevator doors opened, she yanked me out and escorted me into the first office on the left.

"Sit!" she commanded, pointing to a rickety lawn chair in the makeshift waiting room. I did as told and she proceeded through a heavy door with a "No Admittance" sign. The tiny oriental doctor was inside for ten minutes or so before emerging with a flourish.

"Go!" she declared, while holding open the heavy door for me. I arose slightly unsteadily, rubbed my aching arm and trudged into the room behind the door. It was obviously an office for seeing patients, with an examination table, some medical signage on the walls and tongue depressors scattered about the floor and in the sink. There was also a weird black light poster of a hipster having breakfast taped to the back of the door and a polka dot rifle mounted on the wall that didn't seem quite handy enough.

"Hello!" I just about jumped out of my shoes when a man old enough to be my age sprang from beneath the examining table and bounded to his feet right in my face. I was startled but not quite sick to my stomach as he stuck out his hand to shake. I grasped his hand and it was cold, damp and spongy.

"I'm Doctor Ramsey. Well…'doctor'…you know how it goes. Dr. Teng told me what happened with you tonight – and she told me some other things that I guess your wife had mentioned to her before. I'd like to run a series of tests to see if we can't get to the bottom of it."

"Um…well, OK – I guess. But I don't think there's really anything wrong with me."

"We'll just see, won't we?" he said, as he began gathering materials for the impending examination. Dr. Ramsey spread out a picnic blanket on the floor and arranged a collection of candles, mealworms, grape hyacinths, medical audits, Reagan family photos and pericardium into the shape of a bloated Alessandro Manzoni and ordered me to lie on my back in the middle of it. The doctor then leaned over me and roughly crammed a palm full of poppy seeds into my mouth; I felt dizzy and then I guess I must have passed out. All I know is that when I awoke, Dr. Ramsey was leaning against the counter, grinning like an oaf and twirling a string of pasta around in his right hand.

"Young man, I have diagnosed your condition."

"Yeah?"

"Yes I have. You have an affliction that I, in fact, discovered a few years back. It's called "Crazy Head" and you are the fourth person I have diagnosed with this condition. I know it sounds bad but the good news is that it's easily contained with a regimen of medicine and indulgence. There is absolutely no reason why you should not make a complete recovery from this. Let me get your medication set up."

Dr. Ramsey left the room, presumably, I felt, to get a prescription pad or some such. He returned after just a couple of minutes; instead of handing me a written prescription, he reached into the side pocket of his yellowish smock and fished out a baggie with 25 or 30 colorful little pills.

"Here. Take two of these every morning for the next two weeks and you'll be fine."

"What are they?"

"Don't worry about it. Just take 'em and you'll be fine."

So I DID take them and I WAS fine. In fact, I was better than fine. I was euphoric. I felt refined, nimble…supple. I experienced feelings of well being that I not experienced since the backseat power plant incident of 1977. Sadly, however, when I returned to Dr. Ramsey's a couple of weeks later to get more pills, his office had been boarded up tight, with nails and planks and whatnot. A posted sign indicated that a crime had been committed on the premises and that the police had quarantined the area for an undetermined number of months.

The incident with Dr. Ramsey brought to mind a long-ago visit with a Dallas-area medium that told me I would die on October 27, 2028 in some kind of freak fishing accident. I didn't want this information and certainly didn't ask for it, but she shouted it at me when I wasn't quite ready. Still, it wasn't all that bad – 2028 would give me right around the average American male lifespan and I felt that there was much I could do with it – both in and out of my head.

And as I considered it, I began to notice an "out" of sorts. I had not fished since I was a kid and had absolutely zero interest in the activity. It stood to reason that as long as I never fished – especially in October of 2028 – that I would not die in a fishing accident. I told the medium of my revelation but she just shook her head.

"Doesn't work that way. You will die October 27th, 2028 in a fishing accident. There's nothing you can do to prevent it. It's already written. You're a dead man. Just try to enjoy the time you have remaining and try to inhale all that surrounds you."

And so I have – in my mind, on the street and with bells on (as weird as that sounds).

1

Candy Canes, Discipline and the Girl Next Door

THE EARLIEST MAJOR WHIPPIN' I can recall occurred at or around age five, but I'm reasonably certain that there must have been a substantial number even before that. The severity of this particular whippin' and the obviously practiced dexterity of my mother's hands dictates that she had not only done this before, but had essentially perfected it. She somehow managed to drag my blathering four year-old brother and me over a hundred yards – with us tugging and screaming like Little Richard's bearish great aunts – while landing stinging blows to our backsides (23 to me, 20 to my brother, if memory serves).

Not saying this one wasn't deserved… can't say it and I believe it's important that I don't. And I'm not claiming "child abuse", "Dark Ages villager mandate" or anything traditionally predictable. This was the sixties and ideas on the disciplining of children were extraordinarily different than today and even into the near future. Whippins' were not only acceptable, but were often cheered by peeping throngs who seemed to have nothing better to do with themselves and their ugly little things. That these whippins' often occurred outside in the open lends credence to my belief that whippins' were as American as prescription medication. I imagine when parents in the neighborhood gathered at their parties, barbeques, sewing situations, leopard lodges and swinger outings, they compared notes and shared techniques on the dispensing of whippins' and applauded one another's ingenuity, creativity and good ole' common sense.

Supposedly, this particular whippin' was administered due to our lack of responsibility or "preposterous irresponsibility", as my mother so poignantly phrased it. And I won't argue the point much except to say that we were babies. How much "responsibility" can realistically be expected from two children who believed that Peter Sellers had actually married a crippled male porcupine? We weren't bad kids, but we were mischievous and easily influenced. When the bigger though mundanely irrelevant kids beckoned, we followed, no explanation provided or required. We were followers in a naked kingdom of perpetual followers and it usually seemed like a pretty damn good place to be – at least when our tongues were hanging out.

Some of the older neighbor kids – Bobby, Todd, Gordon & Van, I think –sauntered down the crepe myrtle-lined sidewalk toward our house one summer morning as my brother Keith and I were busily constructing bloody, crusted mud pies in the front yard. It had rained a bit the previous day and our yard was barren anyway, so there was a plentiful supply of mud readily available. I preferred a thin, unassuming mud pie; I pounded the mud until it was paper-thin and then adorned it with handles, empty lipstick tubes, custard and even the occasional rusty nail. Keith opted for thick, sloppy mud pies filled with rubbing alcohol, circus peanuts, Sir Walter Raleigh pipe tobacco and orange-flavored baby aspirin. He usually consumed his; mine were strictly decorative and often accepted for show at a local strip mall or beauty supply.

This group – we called them the "Backstreet Boys", we really did – seemed like teenagers to us though in actuality, they were probably just a couple of years older than we were. They were worldly, however, and always seemed to be wearing the coolest bellbottom pants and talking about all these radical kids they knew two or three streets over. One – Bobby, as I recall – had even kissed a girl and described it as "bumpy and sticky with something like sauce and almost pretty nice but not actually in a way". He also claimed that girl's tongues had polyps the size of clenched fists and were scaly like a lost species of dinosaur or possibly marine life. Bobby's family had a talking parrot that was always saying Hail Mary's and quoting Debbie Reynolds and Lady Bird Johnson with a vengeance, though refraining from the use of profanity just in case.

It was also known that this talented parrot could recite the Gospel of Judas verbatim without conveying any sense of detachment, which was troubling to me. Each of the Backstreet Boys had last names though I didn't know them at the time; however, I did know for a fact that none of them had the last name of Piedmont or Ishmael.

They stopped in front of our previously well-bricked house and formed into a kind of a messy football huddle, whispering and looking at us and whispering some more and then looking at us again. Keith and I sat in the mud -- mud pies in hand -- staring at them with the sort of muted anticipation that can end up staining your pants if you're not careful. Keith was wearing an oversized shirt with an embroidered baby duck and black short pants that showed his hiney when he was sitting. And he was damn muddy...damn muddy. I was clad in Dallas Cowboys garb and probably looked a lot like a gravy-stained status hero...and not too muddy though a little bit wet and patently chilly.

"Hey, you guys wanna see a candy cane cave?" Bobby positioned his arms straight out to either side, palms pointed straight up, almost as if he were preaching to a gaggle of assembled followers and Israelites in the role of one of Jesus' thick, ordinary disciples. It was a question, but it was formed as a patronizing challenge designed to insult our youthful intelligence. I believe he was trying to be a situational Billy Graham but he looked and sounded more like a tipsy train conductor in search of some untold truth. Keith and I glanced at each other, confused, and then turned back to the suddenly dancing Backstreet Boys.

"Huh?" we asked virtually, though not quite, simultaneously. It was more like a rapid fire, staccato "Huh-Huh" and probably sounded like coalition air strikes on civilian villages made of adobe."

"A candy cane cave. A cave with candy canes growing in it. Do you wanna see one or what?" Bobby raised his eyebrows awkwardly as if to profess queer confusion at our confusion, and then made a kind of whirling action with his hands as if to demonstrate solidarity with his perpetually staggered universe. At least that's what it looked like to me and I was pretty damn perceptive for a kid my age. I couldn't help but think of Bobby as a professional fiddler with nothing except a tuba to play; he would obviously make the best of any situation but repatriation would be mostly problematic.

"Um...sure," I stammered, sort of glancing back at my house for any hint of adult supervision or scrutiny. No, there wasn't any and that's not a condemnation. Mom must have been ironing or washing or cleaning or something. Maybe she was pontificating. But she was nowhere to be seen which, I deduced, was clearly indicative of her wholehearted approval. Obviously, if she had any problem with us heading off to the exotic land of candy cane caves, she would have barked some harsh disapproval or at least latent opposition. But my lemming shaped ears heard nothing and that was enough for me, at least at that point in time. I grabbed my muddy brother with the faltering pants and the duck on his shirt and found my coat and grabbed my hat. "Let's go!"

And off we scampered right behind the butts of the Backstreet Boys across crumbling Greenland Drive, our destination being a huge open field behind the homes across the street. In current times, this is the site of the LBJ Freeway, the busiest and most important thoroughfare in Mesquite, Texas but back then, it was an overgrown pasture with coves of troubling trees, weeds the size of decent-sized accountants, smelly standing water and, according to legend, coyotes, wolves, snakes, rats, bears, barracudas and Joey Bishop. There were even rumors that this field was the home to three African-American teenagers dubbed by our live-in nanny as "zealous Negroes". The Backstreet Boys called them "Warren Harding" while I just considered them quick with extended muscle tone.

We followed the butts of the Backstreet Boys between two smoking houses, over a faltering chain link fence, through the empty yard and out the unlocked back gate, which had been impaled by a switch. We crossed the narrow paved alley and entered the mosquito-laden field, which I had surmised was likely the home of the candy cane cave and much more. As we plodded into the vast field, we were engulfed in sounds; not wildlife, necessarily, but nature – rustling, flapping, croaking…stuff like that. It's not unreasonable at this point to wonder how kids our age were able to sneak away without the knowledge of our guardians. All I can tell you is this is how it was for everyone -- at least in our little corner of the world. Not only did we leave home; we stole fins, locked horns and even cut our own hair on occasion.

"It's right over there," said Bobby, pointing to a little forest of trees and other swirling unruly growth. He bravely led the way --curled guide stick in hand -- followed closely by his Lieutenant Governor Todd, Captain Half-Speed Gordon and all of their unspoken dreams and aspirations. Van kind of hung back with us; it was clear to me that he had not yet seen the candy cane cave and, on top of that, showed more than a little apprehension at the very prospect. Probably should have been a signal to my brother and I but we dutifully trudged onward through the damp, swaying weeds that rose up out of the mud past our waists and seemed to reach upward for the birds and the clouds.

Without fanfare, we arrived and none of us celebrated it in the open. The mass of trees and vegetation had grown high and intersected overhead, indeed forming a cave, though not in the traditionally stone sense. But it did block the sun and we entered the dark "cave" carefully and not at all assertively. It wasn't pitch black but it was what I like to call a "spooky dark" -- we could peer at stuff but not with much clarity. The ground inside the cave was basically free of grass and weeds, with some discarded wood – maybe pallets, maybe bookmarks – slung about in the mud and muck. Wordlessly, silently we marched into the spooky dark, unworried about ramifications or perceived dangers that might be casually fidgeting or lying in wait.

Bobby's voice rang out, jarring and even scary. "Right there -- look! See it. Right there!" He was pointing up with his guide stick at a sagging tree limb that was hanging down at an awkwardly low level. "Right there!" I looked but at first saw nothing out of the ordinary, just jagged twigs, a few brown leaves, and maybe a hoot owl or two. I think the leaves were brown...could have been beige or even yellow. And the owls struck me as modest, sedate and downright bookish.

"Right where you're looking!" Gordon chimed in with a hint of sarcasm and maybe, as I look back on it, a bit of a stifled chuckle or giggle. He already had unappetizing pimples at his young age and they seemed to be telling an unfortunate story all that was all their own, a story of the downtrodden and the uninitiated (or under-initiated). "Don't you see it?"

Then I did. "No way! Look, Keith, right there!" Astonishingly, I was pointing at a real, packaged candy cane hanging from a real tree limb. The red and white confections were a favorite of mine and I enjoyed sucking them down to a sharpened point -- a point that could probably break skin -- before finishing them off with my clattering and still immature teeth. "Wow!" Keith spotted the candy cane and was clearly entranced, attracted and whatnot.

But there were more, too many to count it seemed (though I doubt I could have counted much past twenty anyway). Candy canes bloomed from limb after limb after limb; everywhere I turned, everywhere I looked candy canes filled my senses. This candy cane cave was really making my day, or so I reckoned at the time. For a five year-old boy, can anything on earth really top a cave full of sprouting candy? At that tender age, the meaning of life is pretty much candy, toys, pooping, running amuck and girl's underwear. Right?

And so it was time for the candy harvesting to begin, despite the fact that it wasn't Valentine's Day or even Tuesday. I had only climbed a couple of trees in my family's backyard at this point in my young life but I felt pretty sure I could do it; my brother, probably not, but I was confident in myself. I had determined that I would share some candy canes with him, I really had. The bark was damp and flaky as I took the trunk by the horns and attempted to pull myself off the stinking, slathered ground.

"Aaaarrrrrgggggghhh!!!!" A high-pitched, piercing and decibel-busting scream nearly knocked my socks off and I mean they almost literally came off. It sounded like Queen Elizabeth or possibly Ernest Borgnine being consumed live by a hungry lion or deranged shark or something similar…it was goddamn scary and that's what I'm here to tell you! I swung my head around in the direction of the noise and witnessed the last several feet of Van's descent as he fell liberally from an adjacent tree. I don't know how high he was…ten feet, fifty feet? Don't know. But he had shimmied quickly up that tree like a real pro or someone else who is proficient at something special. He fell backwards and landed square on his back – HARD, two candy canes still in hand and his pride, I imagine, gravely wounded.

He lay motionless on the ground for a few seconds and I initially thought he might be dead or headed that general direction. But then he leapt suddenly to his feet and began to dance a lil' jig, not unlike something you would see on the Ed Sullivan Show or in Sunday school. It was actually quite entertaining to watch, though a little ragged around the edges and in need of some seriously scripted rehearsal. His arms were flailing erratically above his head and his legs went up, down and around, kind of like a chubby naked Russian dancer on acid, or something more than comparable.

"Beeeeeees!!" He was screaming like a banshee and that's the truth. We all looked at each other. "Bees?" we wondered.

"Beeeeees!!" Then we saw them. He had evidently disturbed a nest of wasps and there were at least a couple of dozen flitting about and around Van. Of course, wasps are not bees, but as kids, we called everything that could fly and sting "bees", whether they were wasps, hornets or something more sinister. Kind of like any soda pop is a

"Coke" and any toasted pastry is a "Pop Tart" and any bottle rocket is a "Black Cat".

I felt a whoosh and a thud or maybe a thunk on my forehead as an attacking wasp swooped past. It didn't sting me but was either sending a warning or marking its territory. Keith was crying like a four-year old; I don't know if he was stung then but I do know that he was stung eventually. The Backstreet Boys, with Van unashamedly leading the way, took off charging back toward the houses on Greenland. I grabbed the left hand of my bawling brother and took off right behind them, limping slightly though I'm not sure why. Several of the wasps chased us for a while, but then seemed to grow bored with the encounter and, I believe, returned to the candy cane cave, hats in hand and smiles all around.

The sight of the wasps was scary but the sight of my mother was scarier. She was standing, hands positioned on hips, in the alley behind the homes, glaring something akin to petulant daggers or poison darts directly at my brother and me. The Backstreet Boys noticed her and purposely went the long way around and I admired them greatly for doing so. She did not seem to notice, her cryptic glare pasted on Keith and me -- mainly me. She was not a large woman but when she was mad, she was intimidating, what with the gritted teeth, trembling hiss and maniacal disposition. She moved at us and was on us in seconds, grabbing us first by the ears and then by our skinny biceps, triceps and associated blades.

Mom yanked us for a few yards and then went into what must have been a rehearsed and coordinated system of releasing my arm to pound Keith's bottom, then grabbing my arm again and releasing his arm to pound my bottom -- then grabbing his arm and releasing my arm to pound his bottom; all the way home this went on! And her whippins' were actually lifting us off of the ground with each impact and I found myself missing the wasps very much indeed. As our little family train churned home, I was acutely aware of neighbors watching, pointing, making sandwiches and selling popcorn. I'm pretty sure the wasps were watching too, from a distance, smiling and judging us probably a little too harshly with their vacuous wasp personas and their trimmed and oily wasp mullets.

Mom escorted us roughly into the house and then things calmed down. She said that we should wait until our Father got home and it was stated as pretty much an unveiled threat. But at least we got the chance to chill out and that was definitely welcome at this juncture. And I got the opportunity to do a bit of five-year old "soul searching", such as it was. It did, at this time, occur to me that at least some of the Backstreet Boys had likely hung the candy canes in the cave. Why? To humiliate a pair of gullible brothers with running noses and grave misconceptions? Maybe. To infiltrate a communal passage between the precious and the systematically unworthy? Well, no, probably not. It was the first bullying I had ever experienced and, as my five-year old mind analyzed it, it was bad but not that bad. Yes, I got physically hurt but I was mainly physically hurt by my mother and not by the bullies. If this was an example of the future of bullying in my life, I was guarded but not all that worried. As Carl Perkins had once famously uttered to Elvis Presley's mother: "When I get home from a long night on the patio, I don't want nothing 'cept a sweet-smellin' line."

When I told the little girl who lived next door about the traumatic experience, she insisted that I memorialize it in poem. I was initially hesitant because of a dull toothache but she kept after me and I eventually penned this ditty:

My brother and me found a candy cane cave,
Its fleece was white as snow.
And when our mother found out about it,
It rocked our status quo.

Our family moved away a short while after the candy cane cave incident. We only moved about three miles but it might as well have been three hundred. I ran across various Backstreet Boys only sporadically through the years, usually in real time. I've heard that one Backstreet Boy became a pharmacist who was found to be on the take and another one actually discovered a new species of lily. He was unable to cash in on his discovery and became relegated to a life on the roof. Another Backstreet Boy was unaccounted for many years until his social network profile popped up one day recently and indicated that a career in professional gambling had gone horribly, horribly askew.

To this day, my mother refuses to acknowledge the incident and my middle-aged brother cries girlishly at the mere mention of it. It has remained in vivid color for me after all these years, probably because of a curiously widening crease in my medulla. It's uncomfortable but it doesn't hurt. It really doesn't.

• • • • • • • • • • • • • • • • • • •

2

Alexander Hamilton and a Greater Good

AFTER MOVING TO OUR new house on Sidney Drive, we did not move again during childhood and I liked that. I always felt bad for the kids whose families moved during the school year. I never had to be the "new" kid at school and I'm glad; I don't think I would have handled it well at all. Anyway, our neighborhood was decidedly middle-class – the homes weren't big and they weren't small – and though my friends on the street tended to come and go, there always seemed to be much in common with whoever was around at the time.

On a dreary and damp Saturday, this kid named Steve and his family moved into the neighborhood, probably about a year or two after we did. I remember that it was a Saturday because all the homes had their Saturday lighting enabled and illuminated. He was my age—I think nine at the time – and despite his queerly thick glasses and missing teeth, I enjoyed hanging out with him. I think he had a younger sister but I don't recall ever seeing her and, looking back, it's conceivable that she was completely made up. I was over there *a lot* and she always seemed to be at the five and dime or the soda fountain or the Mediterranean art shop. Don't remember her name but I do remember that it started with an "L" and sounded like action.

Steve and I used to hang out in his garage drinking an unlimited supply of localized Dr. Pepper. His dad was a delivery driver for the Dr. Pepper company and, for some reason, there always seemed to be stacks and stacks of cases of bottled Dr. Pepper in their garage, sometimes stacked haphazardly but often very neat and orderly. I never knew quite why they were there but I was glad they were. We would sit around, getting DP-buzzed, talking about kids at school or Gunsmoke and playing with his dog "Alexander Hamilton". Alexander Hamilton was a tiny little, white-haired mutt of a dog that liked Dr. Pepper, dead mice and Bill Wyman. Steve named the dog Alexander Hamilton because he felt that, somewhere down history's line, the original Alexander Hamilton should have at some point been our President. It was a tribute, really.

"Only three men in the history of America were as smart as Alexander Hamilton…Einstein, Edison and Ben Gazzara. That's it. Alexander Hamilton was smarter than everyone else and it's a disgrace, a disgrace I tell you, that he was never President". Steve always got worked up when the topic was Alexander Hamilton and I usually attempted to deftly change the subject with a pleasing observation or a crass reduction.

"So, Steve…so what's the deal with Matt and Kitty? I mean, really. She's not getting any younger and he's no real trophy himself, especially his feet. And frankly he doesn't look like he smells very good. I bet he smells like a burned-out benefactor or something…can you just imagine?"

"Well, she doesn't smell very good either, I guarantee you. Hygiene in the old west was bad and she wears the same clothes a lot and they look damp. And in the color episodes, if you look really close, you can see a thin, light film of something horrible on her skin – and you just *know* that couldn't have smelled good. Sometimes it looked like the other actors were averting their eyes when she came spinning through."

"Yeah, stinking Kitty" I agreed earnestly.

One summer morning -- July 15 as I recall -- I showed up at Steve's garage and was taken aback by the sight of a fairly imposing black fellow in the garage with him. This was unusual for our neighborhood and I involuntarily recoiled, at least initially, before steadying myself with special reactionary hands and feet.

"Hi," I stammered sheepishly, looking at my feet as they obviously began to tell a fervent story.

"This is Chandler McDaniel!" Steve spoke excitedly and almost void of irony. "The Dallas Chaparrals? Chandler McDaniel? He plays center for the Chaps! Can you believe he's here?"

I could not. I was a HUGE Chaps fan growing up…the biggest! I listened to every game on my little transistor radio and would celebrate wildly when they won and bawl inconsolably when they lost. My parents were actually worried about the level of my fandom for a while there and strongly considered getting me some semi- professional help at a nearby clinic. Cincy Powell, Glen Combs, Ron Boone, Gene Moore, Chandler McDaniel – they were my frickin' heroes and my love was genuine and unconditional. And here was one of them standing two feet from me, drinking a warm Dr. Pepper and pursing his lips like a madman!

"Hey there, little man." Chandler was shaking my hand but looking over my head at something behind me. I turned out of curiosity and saw that he was looking through the door that opened from the garage into Steve's house. Right inside that door was a little laundry room where Steve's mom was busy ironing and, I think maybe folding and hanging clothes. She was very nice, always fixing us little snacks and such when we were hanging out or even bopping about. She reminded me of Julie Andrews from that "Sound of Music" – looked like her and kind of moved around like her-- though I don't believe she could sing a lick. She always wore these clear cubes with real crickets inside dangling from her ears, which I always thought was really pretty cool and she had a number of dangerous-looking moles on her face and neck (also pretty cool). I couldn't understand why Chandler was so transfixed on a lady bent over an ironing board but was sure he had his reasons. Anyway, I was just thrilled to meet him and wanted to seize the moment with all that I had.

"You got nine rebounds against Carolina. How did you do that? Their center is like seven feet tall and…." I don't think Chandler heard a word. He adjusted his copper bracelet, draped his silver necklace back over his shoulder and strode purposefully into the laundry room behind Steve's mom. He said something into her right ear that made her shudder, convulse and giggle a little and then closed the door behind him without turning around.

"Whew! Chandler McDaniel! I can't believe it!" I was star struck, no question. Still, inexplicably, I was beginning to be overcome with a weird, nagging suspicion.

"Steve, didn't you think he'd be taller?" Sure, he was tall compared to us but I didn't think he seemed all that much taller than my Dad, who was basically an average size man.

"Are you kidding? He's tall, man...really tall. I've seen him on TV. He's tall!"

"What's he doing here?"

"He was just walkin' down the street – Chandler McDaniel walkin' down our street! I was just sittin' here in the garage and he walked up and startin' talkin' to me. I gave him a Dr. Pepper. He's really cool and he knows about a lot of things."

"Yeah, he does," I agreed.

I went over to Steve's the next day and Chandler McDaniel was there again, hanging out in the garage with Steve and Alexander Hamilton. I'm pretty certain he was wearing the same clothes from the previous day -- black tee shirt torn in all the coolest places and brown corduroy trousers with worn knees and mustard stains. I think his white tennis shoes were Adidas because they had three black stripes on the side, but I didn't see "Adidas" printed anywhere and I supposed they could have been a generic equivalent or some such.

"You gotta check out what me and Chandler did last night," said Steve, breathlessly, as he rummaged around in a big cardboard box filled with things and marked "Plaintive" in big black letters on one side. It sounded like flitting chickens in a crowded barnyard as he rustled around with his hands through the items in the box and it began to hurt both of my ears as well as the gross, juicy part of my tubular brain.

"Look!" Steve held up a pretty decent looking gold watch with "Rolex" engraved on the front. "Chandler says this watch is worth $3000!"

"Wow!" I was suitably impressed as I peered over the edge to see the contents of the cardboard box. It was loaded with watches, rings, necklaces, bracelets and all kinds of other bright and shiny objects. I even saw some forks, spoons, mugs, chef hats, pickles and outdated medicine amongst the booty. Everything looked good though some of it didn't shine as brightly as others. "Where'd you get all this stuff?"

"Get this...Chandler took me over to Stallcup Drive. People left their windows unlocked so that we could come by and get their donations to charity. Chandler works with lots of charities."

"I LOVE goddamn charity!" Chandler interjected between extended puffs of something pungent.

"Not all the windows were unlocked. Some people forgot but Chandler had this cool jimmy stick with a hook that opens windows – opens 'em right up!"

"Damn straight". Chandler was through puffing and had moved on to digitally clearing his nose of some kind of irritant or possible obstruction.

It hit me like a ton of something heavy…really heavy. This wasn't Chandler McDaniel, the professional basketball player for the Dallas team – couldn't have been. This was likely an ex-felon or escaped convict who had recruited my friend Steve to crawl through windows and burglarize homes. I was all at once uncertain, frightened, fidgety and indignant. Obviously, this guy could have been dangerous. Did Steve really believe the "charity" load of shit or was he actually in on it? Or, worse, was he being forced to participate against his will?

I didn't know what to do. I had never really been around a criminal before, except for the convicted rapist that worked at the Mite-T-Mart just down from the corner. Well, and my brother Keith who had been caught shoplifting candy at Safeway. And yes, there was my baby brother Mike who had been involved in some kind of ugly scene at the barbershop…but nobody really dangerous. I wanted to tell someone older than me what was going on, but I didn't want to get Steve in any trouble. And I didn't want to be a snitch and I didn't want to get hurt by "Chandler", who seemed more than capable of inflicting pain and suffering on the likes of me.

It was simply too much weight for my nine year-old head to bear. I knew I wanted to do the right thing – but what was really right? In the end, I resorted to a mechanism that would serve me well through the years – I stuck my head in the sand and avoided the situation entirely. I spoke not a word about it to anyone or any teacher. I stopped going over to Steve's and I avoided him like the dickens at school. I even stopped following my beloved Dallas Chaps -- total and absolute avoidance. And you know what? In time it passed.

I would notice "Chandler" for a couple of more weeks when I peered out our front window toward Steve's; then he just sort of disappeared… moved on to his next caper, I suppose. Not long after, three Mesquite police cars spent the better part of a day over there – was never sure what they were doing but they did remove several boxes of items from the garage; one officer, an ample-bellied bear, even tripped and fell flat on his face while crossing the clumpy lawn. I laughed a little bit at that but even then I knew that my laughter was misplaced and mishandled.

Occasionally, I would see Steve's mom, either out in the front yard or going to and from the car, which was always parked on the street curb in front of their house. It was clear that her body was inflating over the months that followed. I wasn't, at that point, all that sure how the pregnancy and baby thing worked but it became obvious that she was going to be culminating a reproduction cycle...and soon.

The baby – a boy – arrived with little or no fanfare that I noticed. I overheard Steve mention it at school and I think I caught my parents discussing it in overtly hushed tones in the front seat of the car at the drive-in hamburger joint. One evening, I was out on the sidewalk in front of another neighbor's house when Steve's mom came walking up toward me pushing an Argentina blue baby carriage. Gosh, it might had been nearly a year since I had spoken to her at that point and she stopped, smiled, said hello, asked how I was doing at school -- she was very nice. And the baby was very black...*very* black.

That was to be the last time I ever saw her. Maybe a week later, Steve was absent from school and two kids in my class – Jason and Jerrold – said that the family was moving away. I came home from school that day and saw a large burgundy and lime moving truck parked sideways in front of Steve's house. Their car was not there and I imagine that they had already gone ahead to their new home, wherever that was. It's funny, but the people in the neighborhood, kids included, never mentioned Steve's family again at all – almost as if they had never existed in the first place. Being just a child and not wanting to make any unnecessary waves, I didn't mention them either, except in code and in song.

3

The Mongolian Vomit Skirmish

IT'S SAD AND EVEN regrettable that my initial inclination was to laugh enthusiastically when I walked into the house from outside and found my nine year-old brother Mike contorted into a fetal position on the couch, moaning like a harpooned Bob Denver. My cool 16 year-old self was unable, at that point, to generate anything in the way of sympathy, empathy or understanding; I just knew that he looked funny and he sounded funny and that spittle escaped my lips wildly as I convulsed spastically into a monumental fit of uncontrolled laughter. My wild guffaws even knocked me off balance momentarily and I grabbed our splintered coffee table for support as I began to tumble backwards onto the creaky, dusty hardwood floor, landing hard on my back like red rover.

My youngest brother was a peculiar sort, competitive to a fault, and demonstratively obsessed with anything from Mongolia and people that were missing limbs or other non-essential body parts. He attempted, at various points, to learn Latin, to march with a precious crew of bootleggers, to bottle his sneeze and to construct his own makeshift paradise. Despite failure on all counts, Mike remained acutely accessible to strange, new challenges and could never be accused of shirking, backing down or lollygagging (in that way that many will).

He and his best friend Bradley were prone to locate mischief, even where there seemed to be none available. The two of them had been known to shut down busy highways, initiate marshal law, penetrate walls of marginal defenses and to create general urban turmoil. Mike and Bradley were accurately identified by titled officials as "havoc-wreakers" and their whereabouts seemed to be monitored at least 18 hours a day by computer and by military radar apparatus. Even still, trouble usually had little trouble finding them, and they it.

Bradley was a stout believer in "survival of the fittest" and had no reservations when it came to the belittlement of the weak, the frail and the "not too bright". If he issued a challenge or directive, he very much expected a desirable response, or at least a reasonable effort. When they combined forces, Bradley and my brother Mike – two suburban baby-faced nine year-old kids – could deal a whole lot of misery to the unsuspecting general public and also to plants, trees, bushes and even unsuspecting sows.

It was an off-the-cuff comment by Bradley that set off a chain of pain and embarrassment for my brother Mike that none of us would never forget. Bradley could boast with the best of 'em and was always claiming to have earned some prestigious award, toppled some muscular gladiator or prevailed in some notable dereliction of duty. For a nine year-old, he was pretty damn worldly and even a cool teenager like me couldn't help but be somewhat impressed. On this particular Friday, Bradley claimed to have consumed a 30-ounce can of peanuts in seven minutes under an hour and further bragged that, upon completing the peanuts, he immediately rode his bike on one wheel to Dairy Queen for a Beltbuster, a Dilly Bar and a smooch from the 18 year-old cashier, who was brunette with blonde highlights and always wore cherry red lipstick on her lips and in her hair.

"Big deal," Mike said, throwing a wadded up ball of paper into Bradley's face. "That's nothing."

"Yeah? You couldn't do it. No way! You're like that song 'Muskrat Love'."

"Like what?" Mike glowered at his friend and began to pop his knuckles. "I'm like that song 'Kung Fu Fighting'. You're like that song 'You Light Up My Life'. Only you're bouncier."

"I'm bouncier?" Brad was warming to this dispute. "Well, I just happen to have a can of peanuts in my lunchbox. Ten bucks says you can't finish it in an hour. I'm not kidding!"

"You're on and I'm not kidding!!"

Maybe had I been there, I could have saved Mike from his maddeningly competitive self. But alas, I was down at the 7-11 playing the Royal Flush pinball machine, a machine on which I had the all-time high score and a machine into which I had inserted hundreds of dollars in quarters over time. My youngest brother was not the type to back down from a challenge – any challenge – and he certainly was not going to let his best friend have the last word on this or any subject. No way.

To his credit (I suppose), Mike finished off the can of peanuts in under an hour. It was an arduous ordeal, complete with tortuous swallowing and graphically audible gastrointestinal gurgling. By the time I arrived home, Brad had already departed, leaving Mike to his own devices, I guess. Yes, I was laughing. I cannot deny this and it would be futile to try. But genuine concern did eventually set in when I began to hear bubbling, percolating and hoarse whispers from the beyond. Involuntary emissions, some of them moist, began escaping his rear and I knew this was serious with a capital "S" and also some other capital letters.

I hurried off to find mother; she was sitting on the bed in her bedroom watching "Perry Mason" and puffing on an unlighted cigarette that was inexplicably smothered in smooth dark chocolate.

"Mom, Mike is really sick."

"He is?" She sat up with a start. "What's wrong?"

"I don't know. But he's making all kinds of nasty noises and the room is stinkin' real bad. He's lying on the couch."

Mom popped up off the bed and walked quickly to the living room. "Michael? Michael? What's wrong, Michael? Michael?"

My brother was unresponsive except for a sad little groan and some ethereal facial tics. His color had changed to a "notebook paper white" and his stomach seemed to be working independently from the rest of his illness-racked body. If it were not so alarming, it would have really been a sight to see.

"C'mon. We're going to the hospital." Mom's voice was unsteady and wavering. She was starting to scare me. "Help me get him to the car. You're driving."

We each grabbed one of Mike's arms, lifted him from the couch, and helped him waddle unsteadily out the front door and into the backseat of my Ford Mustang. He immediately plopped down on his side with his feet still flat in the floorboard, eyes glazing and his anus crackling. Mom rushed back inside to get her purse and whatnot and I sat in the driver's seat, drumming my fingers impatiently on the steering wheel. In thirty seconds, she was bounding back out to the car and jumped into the front passenger seat.

"What hospital, Mom?"

"Doctor's Hospital. And let's hurry up!"

Hurry I did and it was cool to drive fast with parental endorsement. She kept telling me to "go, go, go" and I found myself runnin' about 60 mph on streets that called for 30. Doctor's Hospital was normally a fifteen-minute drive from our house but I was pulling into the emergency room section in something under seven minutes. I really wish I still had that car. It was a 1966 model, baby blue and, in my opinion, snazzy and electric. But, unbeknownst to me, my brother Keith traded it for a broken-down motorcycle and when I found out, I pounded him with both fury and conviction.

We gently lifted Mike from the backseat and escorted him on his wobbly legs into the emergency room. I helped guide him to a seat in the waiting section while Mom went to confer with the giant black lady at the admissions desk.

"How do you feel?"

"Ugh…I feel really sick. I think I ate too many peanuts. But I'm not sure." Mike leaned way back in his chair and closed his eyes, groaning without any real effort. He clasped both hands onto his queerly swollen belly and looked to be pressing down with force to quell something or another. He appeared acutely uncomfortable and I was glad at that point that I was me because I sure did not want to be him.

I covertly surveyed the room and was surprised by the number of people waiting. Straight ahead across an aisle was a pretty twenty-something lady with her arm around a younger sister or possibly a daughter. The younger girl appeared to be in some distress concerning her right elbow and maybe also a knee. I instantly liked the lady – she had long brown hair and wore it swept up and feathered in front. She seemed to have an appealing bosom and was wearing a short skirt which revealed longish, tanned legs. Her face was very nice and I kept thinking she reminded me of someone on television, though I couldn't quite put my finger on it.

On the aisle behind her was a group of five or six bearded and hairy Hispanic men who were wearing filthy uniforms indicative of outside labor. One of them was bleeding profusely from a wound in the neck and was very obnoxious about it. The rest of them were glaring at the pretty lady across from me and conducting coordinated gestures and signals. To my right was a row of chairs backed up against a window that faced the parking lot. There was a father and son; the son was wearing a baseball cap and had a steady flow of mucous streaming from his nose into a self-applied napkin on his chest. The burly father kept his face buried in an automotive magazine with a beaming, bikini-clad woman making a peace sign on the cover. A few chairs down from them sat a stoic nun with a withdrawn, elderly lady who seemed to be laboring. And just down from them was an old, wrinkled man who couldn't suppress his persistent hiccups. This place was not a happy place to be.

Mom came back over and spoke to me in hushed tones. "They're going to see Michael quickly. I know the lady in charge and she is going to see to it."

I had forgotten until then that my mother had formerly worked at Doctor's Hospital, pushing paper across a desk or something. She had worked there until she landed a job in a downtown bank pushing larger paper across a larger desk or something. So, it seems, she was pulling some strings to get Michael advanced to the front of the waiting list. I wasn't sure how I felt about it but looking back, I probably felt a little guilty but also giddy.

"Hey, you better move." Mike had roused to consciousness and was actually speaking to me in complete sentences.

"Huh?"

"I mean it. You better move!" Just then, I saw the look on his pale white face and knew exactly what he meant. As his body began a heaving, massive convulsion, I dove -- body parallel to the ground -- and flew gracefully through the air, landing with a thud in the middle of the aisle and sliding across the tiled floor to a halt at the feet of the pretty lady. I looked back over my shoulder and saw a scene I will never forget: My brother had straightened up in his chair and was spewing a magnificent stream of projectile vomit, shooting straight for at least six feet out in front of him before beginning a gradual descent and splashing triumphantly to the floor.

There were uncontrolled shrieks and gasps in the room as my brother continued his purge without any real interruption. I'm not sure how long it went on...a minute, an hour, I just don't know. What I do know is that the vomit pool – filled with barely digested peanuts, corn, crops and, peculiarly, Halloween costume matter – began to flow throughout our aisle, the next aisle and down a busy hospital corridor.

People were screaming and running about, some in fear, others in perverse bewilderment. It was the largest volume of vomit any of us had ever seen and it was unbelievable that this had originated from a single nine year-old kid. Soon, small children appeared from nowhere and began playing in it and slinging it about -- slipping and sliding and a few even slurping. It's hard to say exactly how much vomit ended up being retched by Mike onto that hospital floor. If I had to quantify it, I would say about five gallons – maybe more, maybe less -- but certainly a lot.

When the spreading began, I had leapt up from the floor, grabbed the pretty lady and the young girl and charged from the room. While pulling them away, I had inadvertently brushed the woman's breast, which was firm and appealing. Once the hubbub had subsided, I went back in to survey the damage. Brother Mike was still sitting there, looking and feeling like a million bucks, smiling and waving me in. I couldn't really get close to him because he was completely surrounded by a literal ocean of vomit -- a literal *ocean* of vomit!

"Aren't you glad I warned you?" Mike was obviously proud of himself.

"Hell yeah I am. So how do you feel *now*?

"Never better. Don't even think I need a doctor now."

"I suppose not." I looked around for any sign of our mother. She had evidently high tailed it for the hills, or somewhere a bit safer and maybe more congenial.

The giant desk lady stepped authoritatively into the room, dragging an obviously reluctant uniformed black custodian behind her. He looked 50, maybe 55 or 65, with a graying beard and a hairline that must have receded rapidly. He wasn't a large man – probably average size and weight – but he was beginning to outwardly resist the huge lady as they came closer and still closer to the project my brother had created for him.

"You kids shouldn't be playing in that," she admonished the half-dozen or so children that were having the time of their lives. "It's nasty. Get out of that right now!"

She turned to the shaking janitor. "Leo, I need you to clean that up."

He just stared back, wordlessly. His stare wasn't an angry stare...it was more of a pleading, long-suffering type of stare.

The giant desk lady was having none of it. "Now! Do your job and clean that mess up!"

Then the poor janitor snapped. "I ain't cleanin' that shit up. Ain't no way! I don't care what the fuck you say. That ain't my job. I ain't doin' it."

The giant desk lady tried to interject. "It *is*..." but he cut her off with a flourish.

"No it ain't! You know what? I don't need this shit. Ain't no job worth this. This is *bullshit*! YOU clean it up! It looks like Fatty Arbuckle threw up that shit. I quit!" With that, the janitor turned and stormed out of the hospital emergency room, looking over his shoulder just once to smirk smugly at the crazed aftermath of my brother's historic illness.

Mom showed back up, as if on cue. "Mike, are you OK?"

"I'm great, Mom. I guess I just needed to puke."

"Alright, let's go then." Mom headed briskly for the exit with Mike and I following obediently. The two of them went out into the day; I turned when I reached the door and gazed back around the foul-smelling room. Most everyone had scattered though there were a few hospital officials standing around, conversing quietly and pointing at the predicament. It saddened me that a man was out of a job because my brother ate a whole can of peanuts. This man had showed up for work that morning, blissfully unaware that his life was about to change forever because of some ridiculous dare that a stranger accepted. I wondered how he would break the news to his family, what he would do to support them. I really wanted to help this man but realized that I was powerless – what could I do? I was just a 16 year-old kid. I hoped that everything would be OK, that he would find a new and better career path that would support his family, pay his bills and help him to lead a fulfilling and successful life.

And I hoped that I would one day be able to forget this spectacle that I had witnessed first-hand. And I also hoped for no more war, I guess.

#4

• • • • • • • • • • • • • • • • • • • •

New Year's Reclamation
and a Thin Blush

I ALWAYS LOVE TO reflect on a particular New Year's Eve, maybe 24 or 25 ago. I was ice-skating on a frozen pond with a second cousin of Audrey Hepburn, conveniently named Anne. Anne was a riot, a true original, and had an obvious knack for coming up with oddball sayings and proclamations that would leave me dizzy and yet somehow thirsty for more. I'll never forget that night, the solemn look on her tubular face, the grave sincerity of her sweet voice, as she imparted her impassioned wisdom.

"If I become wheelchair-bound, don't consider me wheelchair-bound. Consider be subtle."

I was speechless; it is true. What can you say in response to that? I pulled her close, evidently desiring to hug it out. But then my rusting skates gave way beneath me and I fell awkwardly to the choppy ice, clumsily pulling her down with me. Anne screeched a lil' half screech but was not severely injured or anything woeful like that. I was more embarrassed than I was hurt; skating on ice is not easy and it is nearly impossible to stand stationery on ice skates – the human ankle is simply not constructed to perform that act with any level of efficiency. I apologized profusely but, luckily for me, Anne did not hold a grudge.

"Your little moustache is like a helpless lamb in the crosshairs of a strangely land-adjusted Great White Shark...it hasn't a prayer, darling."

"Are you saying you don't like my moustache?"

"No. I'm saying that there is a difference between the truth and the prevailing winds of the Santa Fe ghettos. But the difference can be a cordial one."

I absorbed her intelligence and helped her up from the ice. Anne was no Audrey Hepburn in terms of looks but she was not at all unpleasant. Her face was smooth and cream-colored, her eyes black as a black pillow or black underwear. She wore her pleasantly dark hair down to her waist in the back and, if memory serves, it never really smelled too bad. She was of above-average build in the chest area although her ass was visibly and dreadfully caved-in. Her legs were not long and they were not short – they seemed to serve her purposes quite well. Anne was several years older than me chronologically but light years ahead in experience. She had been around a block or two and I found myself eager to learn lots of stuff from her – I really did.

"Do you see that star?" Anne was pointing to a particular star among the millions of them shining up there in the frigid night sky.

"Which one?"

"The one I'm pointing at – the little blinking star below that group that form the donkey kicking the football."

"Yes!!" Surprisingly, I actually did see the one to which she referred.

"That star symbolizes the truth, struggle and mankind's unsustainable addiction to pleasure. The star can give you hope and it can also give you a kick you in the pants. That star has seen me through tortured times and monitored my early descent into cannibalism. I love it and I hate it but I can never ever ignore it. And I think it wants to father my future child and maybe pretty soon."

I considered this solemnly and then changed the subject. "So... what's Audrey like?"

"She's a wolf, but a likeable one. She takes too many pills and never sneezes except in her movie roles. She eats too much chocolate and smokes too many cigars. She doesn't really keep herself clean anymore and I fear she might have a bad case of shingles or something much worse. But she's Audrey, you know? She has a way about her that will make the back of your neck sting like a thorny bush. And she hates wearing leotards."

I nodded agreeably. "Yeah, that's what I figured." The dark Oklahoma sky began to engulf us and we stood silently next to the frozen pond on ice skates in the rigid grass, lost in our individual thoughts. So what if Anne was no Audrey Hepburn? She was titillating in her own right, arousing me in ways that porno movies could not. She was smart, funny, irreverent and even a bit sassy. Yes, her ass was caved-in but so what? Bulbous, protruding asses were overrated as far as I was concerned. Really, what good were they anyway? Just because her ass was caved-in, did that make her any less desirable? Not to me. Not at that moment. At that moment, the attraction was real and it was *terrifying!*!

"When I make my mark, you will know it," Anne said. "The world will know it. Billboards will proudly proclaim it and pudgy clergymen will fucking herald it. When I make my mark, it will change your world and it will change Ted Knight's world."

"Ted Knight?" I interrupted, but Anne was not fazed and just continued on.

"The gathered masses will consult me on their winding road to salvation, freedom and whatnot. They'll seek my approving gaze and my infantile touch. They'll look to me for answers that I may or may not have. What I cannot answer with honesty, I will fake. I will convey to them the things they want to hear and then send them on their silly way, ever hopeful for the fulfillment of their long-term potential. When I turn to dust, I turn to dust…nothing more".

We gazed at each other kind of blankly for a short while. Then I leaned in and kissed her, planted one smack on her lips. She kissed me back with enthusiasm and tremendous haste. Her breath reminded me of ravioli or something pasta-based, which was OK because I've always enjoyed ravioli and pasta. Her lips felt like lumpy velvet and they seemed more than capable of a little quivering action, which made mine quiver in response. We kissed for three long minutes before I released the lock of our lips. I opened my eyes and hers were already opened wide, silently barking commands at my attentive nose and forehead.

"How was that for you, darling?"

My brain was scrambled and convoluted and could not locate an immediate response, though my groin area was beginning to display obvious signs of approval.

"I...um...that was, uh...I." I stammered nonsense and looked out over the top of her head, searching for something, anything tangible.

Anne sighed deeply. "I know what it is you're going through. Your mind is not artful; it doesn't possess the inner workings to escape, to surrender. It's a feeble mind and is uncomfortable in its own skin."

"I don't think it's feeble," I protested but she put her fingers to my bloody lips to shush me forcefully.

"Ah, yes it is. It's feeble and wayward. It doesn't know this from that and it loses its star power on weekends and in stressful situations. I know the condition all too well and I have the bottled remedy for what ails you."

Before I could say anything, she flexed at the knees, pulled down my sweatpants and began an impassioned manual stimulation of my area. It was surprising but very pleasant; she worked quickly and inserted her own vocalized moans, groans and words of support. I liked what she was doing very much indeed and verbally encouraged her continued efforts on my behalf.

"We'll leave this part out of the biopic of my life," she said grinning shyly and obviously warming to her task, using hands and fingers adroitly.

A throaty "Uh huh", was all I could manage in response.

Despite the frigid air, it was achieved in less than five minutes. Anne stood back up and faced me, beaming with satisfaction at her well-completed task. I was still attempting to regain my composure and found my breathing to be labored and uneven. Anne sought to reassure me in her finest pardonable style.

"When I say that I need you, I'm really saying that I need myself to be mass-induced. I need gongs and filters and patches and pralines and all of the things that indicate rampant underestimation. I need to know the ceiling of my exhilaration. That way, I can password-protect it from the likes of you." Anne was staring into my nose as she spoke, searching for something laudable or crusty, I think.

"That was great...really great," I said. "You are *really* good with numbers...really good."

"No, it's not great," she explained. "That kind of physical act –it is all a vicious lie. Everything about it is a lie. And you know what? It's more of a lie than you'll ever know. You would have no comprehension of a lie at this extreme level. I can only tell you it's a lie and you'll simply have to take me at my word."

"How do I know you're not lying right now?"

"You would know – trust me. If I'm lying with words, the macabre nature of my personality would inflict untold torture and punishment – and swiftly, too. No, my words are true. But that thing I just did is a big, fat lie."

"OK…well, lie or no lie, that was awesome. And I would love to take things to the next level, ya know?" I took her hand in mine and began caressing it lightly. It was still warm from the rubbing and was also curiously small.

Anne adjusted her gaze from my nose to my eyes. "That can never happen. Life works in a certain way and my life works in certain others. If you were to penetrate me with that, I would never allow you to extract…come hell or high water. You would be uncomfortable with the permanence and I would feel guilty at your expense. Romances are nobody's business except for the people involved and their attendants. I simply cannot allow it."

She paused for a few seconds. "Do you want to skate some more?"

I *did* want to skate some more. The two of us glided across and around the frozen pond, forming little circles and doing rudimentary tricks, jumps and kicks. There were no further words spoken – there was no need. I already knew that I would never see Anne again. But her effect on my life was more than a kiss, an embrace or a singular orgasm. It signaled a revolution in my head that herded me down a non-crowded and poorly defined path. A few months later, I heard from this guy named Ted Stegall that Anne moved everything to Guyman, Oklahoma to pursue a career in the art of tree trimming. I was sad, true, but I couldn't help but be impressed by the sheer audacity.

I'm not sure whatever became of Anne. I would imagine that she eventually settled down with a man or husband and satisfied him with her intelligence and with the dexterity of her motion…and hopefully he was tolerant of her caved-in ass. That New Year's Eve remains deeply etched into my medulla and I often find myself wondering what might have been, what might have been. To this day, I sometimes gaze at the little blinking star below the donkey kicking the football and wonder if it's actually possible for a star to father a human child. Science says "no" but the credible Anne seemed to think "maybe".

#5

Basking in a Cool Breeze While Standing Atop a Pygmy

FROM MY EXPERIENCE, GRATIFICATION is not always conventional; in fact, it most often isn't. To rely on standard forms of gratification is to neglect literally millions of opportunities that are out there lurking. For instance, when I heard a local rapper rhyming about the joy of basking in a cool breeze while standing atop a pygmy, I was at first incredulous and then unmistakably curious. Could it be? Could this be somehow strangely pleasurable? Of course, I became obsessive about unearthing the answers because I seem to become obsessive about almost everything

I hoarded my money for a year – living on popcorn, hot sauce and Tab – and eventually found myself in position to afford a flight to Africa. I had heard through some grapevine or maybe a chat room that there were pygmies in Africa and plotted to begin my search in Rwanda, just outside the city of Kigali. From a couple of informants, I learned of a thriving river, along which resided a village of good-natured pygmies. These pygmies were supposedly consumed with affection for lemons, facial cream, ice skates and Neil Diamond and reportedly coveted the lifestyle of true westerners. This seemed like a pure place to begin and I carved the path into my cardboard diagram with a pair of bloody garden shears.

The flight from Texas to Rwanda was smelly and arduous and I wondered if it would ever end – and if it did end, would it be right? I shared a nationality with only a handful of the plane's occupants and I heard enduring snippets of conversations in at least a dozen distinct dialects. The pilot spoke in English but I was not at all comfortable with several of his directives, which seemed brusque and captious. For instance, at one point early on, he came on the loud speaker and informed us that he was "not quite God...but closing in". A bit later, he announced to us that we better keep our goddamn principles to ourselves. The shocked look on the passengers' faces told a story, though I'm not thoroughly sure what. So I simply shook my parted hair, bobbed my head and attempted to display a look of amused annoyance.

Landing in Rwanda was pretty much cathartic, it really was. As I exited the plane and entered the airport terminal, I found that I was enjoying myself very much indeed. There was a snack bar that served tacos, liquefied crickets, paraffin and, I believe, call girls. There was a newsstand with newspapers from all over the world, People Magazines, pencils, nasal spray and disassembled weapons. I saw families reunited and business relationships cemented. The smell inside the airport was pretty ugly but it was still a vast improvement when compared to the odor on the plane, especially during the latter stages of the flight. The lingering medley of perspiration, incense, animal hair and human urine had made sleep impossible and forced me to choke down a meal while holding my nose with parts of both hands.

Out in front of the airport terminal, I hailed a taxi with the gusto of four or five solidly built men. The cab that pulled up to me sounded rickety and sick; the driver looked like Stalin except for a rainbow wig and dangling loop earrings. I told him that I wanted to go to the village of good-natured pygmies by the river.

"Are you a scientist? A doctor?" The cab driver's voice was booming, alarming.

"Um...not in so many words."

"What does that mean?" he roared, mystified. "OK, how many words?"

"Listen, I was really hoping to get a nap on the drive over..."

"How was that smell on your plane?" he interrupted.

"Oh, God! It was freaking unbelievable! It smelled like a combination of incense, perspiration, animal hair and human urine. Rank!"

The driver just smiled and I became all at once aware of what a splendid aroma he maintained inside his cab. I didn't see any visible air fresheners but I detected scents of vanilla, cinnamon, parsley and petunias. It was actually quite delightful and I thanked him for his attention to this detail.

"Just lay your head back and relax, sir. You'll be carousing with the pygmies in an hour." His tone had become soothing and the words were abundantly clear. I was elated for the respite and my eyelids alternated between heavy and lustful, which caused the drive through the countryside to pass expeditiously.

"There it is." The driver was pointing ahead to the right at a cluster of canvas shelters that resembled the teepees of the American Indians. There were a few pygmies scurrying around among the tents, along with dogs, hens and semi-tough decisions. He pulled the cab up to within a few feet of the encampment and half a dozen pygmies approached without any hint of hesitation and surveyed me with fascination etched on their unsmiling faces.

The cabbie explained to me that these pygmies had possibly never seen a Westerner before. I stepped out of the vehicle with my canvas bag slung over my shoulder and leaned into the window to pay for the ride.

"Do you have any advice for me?" I asked as I handed over the American money, which he was glad to accept.

"Don't drink the water, don't fall asleep, and don't quote Hemingway." He was chuckling and combing his rainbow wig as he pulled away.

So there I stood among a growing brood of African pygmies who didn't speak my language – didn't seem to speak *any* language. They sniffed and shuffled their tiny feet a bit but no sound emitted from their mouths…yet. The pygmies seemed fixated on my face and a couple of them even reached up to pat and stroke it inquiringly. I found it odd that most of them looked the same, with skin as black as burnt roast, four feet of stature and rigid, protruding bellies that did not jiggle in the least. They had tied strips of cloth around their waists to conceal genitalia and I was positively pleased about that.

To experience the gratification I was seeking, I needed to select an adequate pygmy. Since they all looked alike and they were all mainly silent, I kept thinking about the Irish Potato Famine, which I realized was eerie. I wiped the Irish Potato Famine clean out of my mind and took the hand of a pygmy who couldn't keep his hands off my face. It was "go time".

I led this particular pygmy, who I nicknamed Art, over to a clearing away from the remainder of the curious group, which had swelled to over twenty. I think that I had asked him his actual name and he responded with something that sounded like "sumptuary law" – which I knew couldn't be right. I took him by the shoulders and laid him carefully onto his back in the dirt (which smelled like febrifuge). The febrifuge-smelling dirt must have been comfortable because Art seemed to really enjoy lying in it – which was not all that bizarre.

It was time. I removed my shoes (Adidas Sambas, as I recall), took a deep breath and thought about the Underwood Tariff Act, though not for long. Hesitantly but in a way matter-of-factly, I placed my left foot atop the apex of the belly which, even with Art on his back, protruded weirdly up into the air. Meticulously, I shifted my weight to my "plant" foot and carefully swung my right foot up next to my left. And there I was, wavering a little but for the most part stable, standing on the belly of this surprisingly accommodating pygmy, with my arms extended out to either side for the expressed purpose of balance.

I felt the breeze; it wasn't exactly cool but it wasn't warm either. For a breeze on the continent of Africa, I regard it as pretty damn nice. I closed both eyes and found myself drifting off to a land of greasy fried chicken, strawberry margaritas and scores of beautiful women who aimed for nothing but to please. It was, of course, Nirvana – an offensive, unhealthy, white trash Nirvana with the glossiness and allure of a thousand strip clubs stacked one on top of the other in a queer series of boxed piping.

I'm not sure how long I perched atop Art's belly, as I unknowingly lost track of time and place. Was it ecstasy? Pretty close. Was it an orgasmic experience? No, though it seems to have been something to build on. As I tried to recall the last time I had felt that good, it became obvious in my head that it was definitely not a weekly occurrence.

I was reluctant to dismount but I knew that I should. I opened my eyes to see that the growing collection of pygmies had crowded in very close, many of them touching Art and me with antique coins and raw fish. They were hooting like fans at a European football match and possessed a craze in their expressions that signaled to me that I had to get away – and quickly! My smile was half-baked and my gaze was zealous as I stepped off of Art and snaked professionally through the throng, many of them grabbing my hands and slapping my back as I brushed past. The crowd had parted behind me and I turned and looked back to see Art, still lying on his back but now spitting blood like some kind of amorphous beast or broker.

Did I feel rotten? Yes, increasingly so. But survival instincts had kicked in and soon I was sprinting from the encampment like a frightened fascist, already replaying the montage of recent events in my head for the sheer enjoyment of it. I easily outdistanced my pursuers but the cab was long gone and I was unable to find any help. So I located a flat, dry place to sit and speculated on the perils of a democratic society, cracking my knuckles for effect. Then I vomited but not much came out.

#6

● ● ● ● ● ● ● ● ● ● ● ● ● ● ● ● ● ●

Ghandi Cronies: Today, Tomorrow and the Day After That

THE MOST INTERESTING PERSON I ever knew in *this* world was a guy named Horst something. Horst and I were in our mid-twenties at roughly the same time but that is where the similarities ended. He had already accomplished a myriad of impressive feats by this point in his life, whereas I had done essentially zip. He once told me that he wrote that jingle for Bain de Soleil tanning lotion, the one that goes "Bain de Soleil for that Central Bay Tan". Horst also claimed credit for writing the line about Secret Deodorant, the one that went "strong enough for a man but made for a woman". He provided guitar lessons and swimming lessons to pedophiles and criminals, despite the fact that he had no idea how to actually play guitar except for light strumming and posing. Horst discovered an improved vaccine for meningitis and developed hosiery that made all women's legs look like Cheryl Ladd's without the use of paint or shipping articles. He had an astute eye for great art and the ability to heal his own broken bones with a heating pad and a dirty eye patch.

We hung out a lot during those days, getting drunk and making fun of the passing simpletons. I knew Horst well but was taken aback when he informed me of his next huge project. He'd become obsessed with the life of Mahatma Gandhi and wanted the world to know all about it. He loved Gandhi's sense of style, the way he moved, his unexplained affection for bleeding raw fish. Horst saw Gandhi as maybe the next "big thing", what with the emotional overtures and calculated banding strategies. Gandhi was what people "in the know" called a "holy man" and commoners had flocked to him from miles and miles away carrying only the shirts on their backs and flip flops.

Horst's plan was to become an American Gandhi-like figure in hopes of inspiring good will and fortune amongst the rabble. He would legally change his name to "Ghandi", spelled in such a way as to avoid legal problems and whatnot. He would wear flowing robes and sandals and would rub various greases on his face and body to sabotage his complexion and skin texture. He would recruit a group of disciples to tour the country with him to spread the language of caring, helping and sugary sweet goodness. They would travel for a year and then Ghandi planned to write a book about the experience, to be entitled "Ghandi Cronies: Today, Tomorrow and the Day After That". Horst laid out his plan the way a big time CEO presents a considered agenda for the weekly staff meeting at the sanitary office.

"So...do you wanna go? Do you wanna be a crony?"

"Are you crazy? Horst, I can't go away for a whole year! That's nuts! And it doesn't even sound like any fun."

"It's not supposed to be fun," Horst retorted, perturbed. "It's designed to help people, to *inspire* people. I'm not doing this for me. I'm doing this for millions and millions of lost souls. I want to save mankind. Don't you get it?"

"No, Horst, I really don't. How are you going to afford to travel for a year, with an entourage, when you won't even have a job or money? How are you going to survive? How are you going to eat?"

"The land and the mountains and the missions will provide. And I'm thinking we won't even have to shave or bathe that much."

I thought Horst had lost his freaking mind, I really did. And I was pretty sure that this moronic idea of his would soon lose all appeal to him. But then it didn't. Horst found a sympathetic lawyer the next day that assisted him in the legal change of his name to "Ghandi". And he recruited a group of willing subjects or "cronies" – Ross, Weldon, Roland, David, Milton and Jerry. The merry band purchased an old used passenger van for $1200 and painted "Cheers!" on the side in block lettering and surrounded it with cool stars, birds, snowflakes and twisted eels. The cronies pledged devotion to Ghandi and swore to follow him wherever his continually updating vision took them. They believed in the man and they believed in his crazy expedition. Was I a *tad* envious? Yeah, maybe just a little. I wasn't envious of the trip or the task but I sure would have liked the freedom to take off and do *something*. I felt anchored to a desk and an apartment and a tiny car and a faintly familial obligation. I thought that, at the very least, the group would have a great story to tell. And, as it turned out, they did.

Ghandi sensed my little disappointment and pledged to include me in the endeavor, promising to mail me a letter every day to update me on their travails. "You'll be with us in spirit but you won't be dead or anything." It was a generous and thoughtful gesture on his part and I was enormously appreciative. I met them in the parking lot of a Skaggs Albertson's grocery store on a brisk Sunday morning in November and helped them load up their fairly hazardous looking van with the items that were needed for their trip. And there was a LOT of stuff and some of it made no sense to me. Why did they need condoms? Or Chef's hats? Or water hoses? Or life-size plastic horses? Or a map of nuclear reactors? Or butt plugs? Or joke books? Maybe they had their reasons and I just could not fathom them. But I dutifully helped pack everything into the van and then watched as they each climbed in and took off down Town East Blvd heading to the interstate and the desired adventurous freedom.

It was three days later when I got the first missive from Gandhi. They had traveled out I-20 west to I-10 in western Texas and then had trekked across New Mexico and ended up in Tucson, Arizona. The group located a nice weekly rate motel and all piled into a single room, determined in their hearts to change the world. They had actually found themselves a little bit of trouble in Tucson; one of the cronies had been arrested for shoplifting a pocket comb from a convenience store and Ghandi had gotten into a dispute over a bad haircut and was slightly injured in the subsequent punch up. Despite the unfortunate incidents, the group was able make sleeve bands for an area cheer squad and picked up litter along an absolutely trashed desert roadway.

Two days later, another letter arrived. Ghandi described their drive from Tucson on to Carlsbad, California. The group overcame a flat tire in Yuma and some translation issues with border patrol agents in California. They ended up at a La Quinta in Carlsbad because two of the cronies were going nuts to visit Near East Land, an amusement park situated up on a hill. The whole gang went to the theme park but problems cropped up immediately when one crony was accused of peeking into the women's restroom and another stole some eyeliner and a can of soup. Ghandi himself got into a fight with a park employee because he was dissatisfied with the length of one of the rides. The group was ejected from the park and Carlsbad police detained them briefly under a notice of entitlement before sending them on their way.

Letters from Ghandi continued to arrive every few days detailing their escapades and accomplishments and even their sleepy moments. They traveled up the California coastline through Los Angeles and into the San Francisco area. They actually got jobs in San Francisco since they had pretty much exhausted their funds by this point in the trip. The jobs entailed murdering animals for fur and nailing protection onto the soles of damaged shoes. Two cronies were fired early on for peeking into women's restrooms, while another was awarded "Employee of the Month." Ghandi dislocated his shoulder in a sparkling blue accident and later filed a grievance with the Governor's office, which was ultimately disregarded and swept away in a calculated manner.

Seattle became their next stop as they found a quiet Days Inn on a traffic circle that served their purposes well. The gang donated sunglasses to the needy and made guitar noises with their mouths to entertain patrons at an area shopping mall. Ghandi may have gotten a Starbucks barista pregnant and a crony got some emergency dental work done at a free clinic that overlooked a bay. Seattle was civil and thoughtful and the cronies felt like they could have settled there permanently. However, Ghandi was increasingly agitated about the clinging barista and insisted that they move on quickly and decidedly.

The letters kept coming as they toured from city to freaking city: Boise, Helena, Salt Lake City, Denver, Fargo...they moved deliberately about, doing some good things and getting into some trouble as well. The trouble was nothing too serious, mind you, but a couple of cronies were arrested for various indecencies and Ghandi had to be pepper sprayed in Fargo after an incident involving hand lotion and a faded photo of the Unabomber. That actually made national news and the television showed Ghandi wearing a sweater vest over his robe while handcuffed, and screaming about his falling arches and his pulsating pupils.

The gang bounced along the northern section of the U.S. – Minneapolis, Milwaukee, Chicago, Cleveland...even Detroit. A crony got married and was left behind in South Bend with a wife and several new kids. Another tried fishing from a private pier on Lake Michigan and caught nothing but a song. Ghandi made his peace with God on a daily basis but could not pass a casino without feeling the need to indulge. He always seemed to be grabbing women's boobs and thrusting himself from behind, secure in the element of surprise. Occasionally, this opened some doors for him but, more often than not, it just resulted in fines, handcuffs and broken hearts.

In New York City, Ghandi wrote to me about a downtrodden black rapper that he had befriended. They met at the base of the Statue of Liberty and the rapper told Ghandi that despite a single hit in the early eighties, he was unable to locate his muse. After a minute or so of deliberation, Ghandi determined that the rapper's problem was that he only wrote songs about architecture and poop. Audiences had evolved and this young rapper had failed to evolve with them. Ghandi encouraged him to broaden his literary horizons a bit and to write songs about things that inspired him, events that affected him profoundly.

Ghandi's pep talk excited the excitable rapper and he had retreated back to his markedly barren apartment that very night and wrote an entire album's worth of raps. He called Ghandi the next morning and invited him to the "Pay Per Play" recording studio on the corner of Macon & Bishop, anxious for my friend to hear his sudden creative output. Ghandi found his way down to the studio and the young rapper met him at the double glass doors in front, smiling, laughing and hugging on him.

"You are da man, Mr. Ghandi, know what I'm sayin'? You showed me da way! Wait 'til you hear dese songs I wrote. I'm gonna be huge!"

Ghandi was delighted at the rappers newfound enthusiasm. He had gone to the studio alone, without any cronies, unaware of what to expect or what to wear. The rapper led him through a maze of narrow hallways that fed into a tiny little control room overlooking a studio strewn with instruments, fast food wrappers and well-deceased insects. In the control room, a balding, paunchy, bespectacled, middle-aged white dude was twisting some knobs and making patronizingly silly faces.

"Steveo, man, I want ya to meet my inspiration. This is Mr. Ghandi from Texas. Mr. Ghandi, this is Steveo, the goddamn best producer the world has ever seen."

Steveo and Ghandi exchanged pleasantries and curious looks. Neither really seemed to belong at this place and both seemed acutely aware of it.

"So, 'Ghandi'," Steveo said, using his voice inflection to artificially mock the name, "My man here says you are the reason for the season… the burr in the saddle…the motor in the home."

"Nah, I just encouraged him to look inside of himself. I don't think young folks do that nearly enough. He really seems like a truly special young man. He just needed to believe in himself."

The rapper could not contain his energy any longer and interrupted. "Ghandi, check dese out, man. Dese are my songs. You gonna freak, man." He handed Ghandi a red notebook stuffed with scribbled-on white lined paper.

Ghandi began thumbing through the pages and actually became more than a little mortified. The songs were entitled, "Beat that Bitch," "My Old Lady Gonna Die," "I Don't Need No Punchin' Bag Cuz I Got My Bitch," "Drug Her and Plug Her," "My Bitch Ain't Good For Nothin' 'Cept BJs", "I Got a Gun and Like to Pistol-Whip Bitches," "Back Up Dat Ass," and "I Made a Mess in My Pants Cuz of You." Ghandi scanned the lyrics and they were full of F bombs, bloodied women and sexual depravities and perversions. He began to get nauseous at the thought that he may have been part of the inspiration for this evil output.

"Mr. Ghandi, I'm gonna go down to da studio and start layin' dis shit down. Wait 'til ya hear me!"

Ghandi had "failed smile" on his ruddy face and mumbled something about breakin' a leg. The rapper disappeared through the doors leading into the studio and Ghandi did not waste a single second turning and sprinting back up the narrow hallways, out the front double glass doors and onto a busy New York sidewalk. I could only imagine what a spectacle it was with Ghandi sprinting like Carl Lewis, robes flowing in the breeze and sandals plopping musically onto the concrete. He made his way back to the hotel, gathered his cronies into a shared semi-circle and spoke of God's judicious manner and the need to hit the road without delay. And so they did.

The six-month mark found the gang in Charlotte, North Carolina occupying an abandoned house on Wilkinson Blvd. Ghandi wrote of the admirable spiritual growth of his clan of cronies and some had even learned to pray with bowed heads and closed eyes. Charlotte was the former home of one of the cronies and he led the gang on an elongated tour of the city's monuments while he was drinking too much rum. The rum went to his head and the tour was ended abruptly by the antics of a gay man who had escaped from a wholesale buyer's iron clench.

Charleston, Atlanta, Jacksonville, Pensacola…the cargo van kept chuggin' from stop to stop carrying Ghandi and his cronies to new frontiers and habitats. Sometimes the cronies found woe. On various occasions, cronies got into fistfights with children, set fire to occupied structures, transformed lap dances into something *much* more and stole contact lenses directly from the eyes of the owners. Ghandi himself had possibly impregnated four women (two of whom were married to each other), broken the leg of a magistrate, transformed a live cat into runny soup and fractured one of his skull bones on a riverboat's propeller.

But the gang had done so much good! They had overseen a controlled bloom of off-color daisies, donated sperm to widows in need, helped a group of Girl Scouts to earn awards for character and quasi-wired an outmoded mental hospital for DSL. They wrote imploring letters to local newspapers and lent their breath to the cause of warming insidious vagrants and their offspring. They had sewn for the poor and shaved the backs of old men who couldn't reach around like that. Each of the cronies felt fulfilled, needed. They were getting to know *themselves* and liked what they had found.

Birmingham, Chattanooga, Nashville, Memphis…the cities started all running together in their heads. Pitifully short of money, the gang got jobs trapping coyotes near an affluent neighborhood. They found trapping coyotes to be more than fun and they took to kicking and surgically probing the offensive animals. When the animals protested, the cronies introduced boiling water to the process and, I imagine, the affluent neighborhood was eternally grateful.

The journey ended with their arrival back in Mesquite, 11 months and six days after their departure. There was, of course, one less crony because Milton had gotten married and stayed behind in South Bend with his new family. They all looked unhealthy and thin, with pockmarked faces and lying eyes. Were they diseased? You could probably say that they were. But their spirits were high and they really smiled a lot…I mean *a lot*!

Ghandi gathered the group around him while I loitered on the periphery, straining to hear the address. "Gentlemen, you have done me proud. What we have accomplished will ultimately change the way that all goodness is gauged. We brought joy to the deserving and the unsuspecting. We helped those in need and led them from the abyss by example. We became better people and better brothers. We meddled when necessary and we raised the standards of the small and the weak. We touched the lives of thousands with our compassion, our wit and even our stinking sore throats. My mind is comforted and my heart is warmed. You are the most important people in my life. I will remember you forever but will never see or speak to any of you ever again."

Ghandi paused, eyes watery, chest heaving. "And I'm keeping the goddamn van."

"Ghandi Cronies: Today, Tomorrow and the Day After That" was eventually published a couple of years later by a collegiate press -- it sold 113 copies. After being hit by three paternity suits and a defamation of character charge, my friend Ghandi was never quite the same. He found work in the tollbooth industry and joined a gym that specialized in unseemly feet. He would come by my apartment every couple of weeks but usually just lounged morbidly on the couch, sometimes speaking in gibberish, sometimes not speaking at all. I fed him beer and nuts and he always consumed greedily, like a starving cocker spaniel.

To me, it was like his purpose in life had been served and he no longer felt the need to participate in any aspect of society. My friend Ghandi became a bit of a lost soul, sadly spinning his wheels and going absolutely nowhere for nobody. When I heard from former crony Roland that Ghandi had passed away from an aggressive sneeze, I wasn't surprised and I really wasn't all that sad. He was actually a very lucky man, having accomplished his life's goal early on, and I imagine he was more or less ready to die and whatnot.

And wouldn't you know it? He willed the van to me along with a sealed envelope, which I didn't open for many weeks. Curiosity finally got the best of me and I opened the damn envelope. Inside was a folded piece of typing paper with words in Ghandi's unmistakable handwriting:

"My morality is my own. I can shape it, nurture it or watch it flop around like a listless dolphin on the floor of a day-old bread store. Sometimes my morality is rowdy and I am forced to chain it to something sturdy. Also, my morality likes raisins, which drives me effin' crazy."

7

Mad Science and the Mother of Invention

I'VE HAD LOTS OF great ideas through the years, I really have. I thought up Smart Phones, electric cars, E-Commerce, Blood Glucose test strips and The Weather Channel long before they ever really became reality. I was always gifted in terms of imagining the ideas but never had much of a clue on how to put them into the marketplace for the gratification of the general public and their favorite nuns. My greatest idea, however, was never realized by anyone and to this day stands unused, not marketed and even somewhat discarded, if you want to know the truth.

This was the late eighties and I was sitting in a bright Baskin Robbins at a table by myself, eating a mint chocolate chip ice cream cone and attempting to eavesdrop on the white couple sitting two tables away. I was curious because the lady was really hot and the dude was portly and frankly funny looking; I needed to understand the attraction. I knew they were a couple and not relatives or simply friends – they held hands for much of their time at the table and I spied him caressing her far too high on her inner thigh under the table. My hearing was great back then and much of what they said was coming through loud and clear.

"My wife thinks you're a whore," the dude says to his beautiful blonde girlfriend. "She thinks you probably give it up to truck drivers at truck stops."

"Your wife is an imbecile. She's probably giving it up to all of your neighbors -- even that old mailman with the goiter." The lady threw her head back, hair slapping the back of the chair, and started cackling with only a modicum of control.

The man was laughing, too. "Yeah, he probably sticks that goiter up her ass." They fiddled with their ice cream sundaes and made eyes at each other. She was such a beauty that I imagined he must have money, power or something else excessive. There was something hanging precariously out of his nose and, for whatever reason, she seemed to ignore it.

"Tell you what, baby," the lady said. "When we leave here, we'll go back to my place and pretend it's a truck stop and pretend you're a stinking truck driver."

"I'm gonna drive something at you. I'll be your bear and you'll be my stylist." I could actually hear his breathing getting heavy and it was making me less and less comfortable.

At that point, sitting in a mostly-deserted Baskin Robbins, it hit me. What if I could invent a spray or even lotion that transformed any ole ho into Sandy from "Grease" before she commanded, "Tell me about it, stud"? If I could somehow come up with a product that chemically altered brain communication or stimulation in such a way, I could be rich and I could effect positive change for tens of millions of hapless sluts. Obviously, the key would be to transform the male's thought processes and that's not always an altogether easy thing to accomplish. Men are predisposed to see the female whore in a certain light and to use the female whore under predetermined and clinical circumstances. I would basically need to manufacture an element that would essentially cross wires in the male brain to precipitate a sufficient reversal of opinion on a "loose" woman.

I sprinted out of the Baskin Robbins, anxious to get home to my "lab" to begin experimentation. Figuring out where to start was a toughie; I've never really had a head for science or math and my work ethic has often been the subject of debate among those in my inner circle. But I had a bubbling enthusiasm for this project and decided that "trial and error" gave me my best chance at a successful outcome.

My bathroom medicine cabinet seemed the best place to start, it really did. A "mad scientist" I am not; in fact, I seldom even get aggravated or miffed. But I began mixing and matching like a wild man, hoping to hit on just the right combination that would help whores appear wholesome. I first combined a few ounces of bismuth liquid with six crushed melatonin tablets and then tossed in a dash of isopropyl alcohol. Then I added a few tablespoons of corn syrup, a squirt of fungus cream and a half-cup of warm buttered whiskey. I beat this into a kind of paste and then went upstairs to see my skinny thirty-something female neighbor that I had met only once. Based on the foot traffic of the variety of guys that were always heading up there, I imagined that she would make an appropriate test subject for my brand new creation.

I knocked twice on the door and she answered in a few seconds.

"Hey, I'm your neighbor from downstairs. I wondered if I might have a minute of your time."

"A minute? If a minute is what you need, you may have it." My neighbor was grinning broadly. I think her name was Tara and she was a couple of years older than me and not all bad to look at. She was extremely thin in all areas and her skin was a pale, pale white. Her hair was dirty blonde, her face was ordinary but she had a surprisingly nice smile, exhibiting tortuously straight white teeth – so straight that I wondered if they might be fake. Tara wore a thick gold sweatshirt, navy sweatpants and no real shoes to speak of. She stood back to allow me to enter and pushed the door closed behind me.

As I glanced around her apartment, I was immediately distracted by several pieces of artwork nailed to the walls behind a sofa and right next to a tall wooden bookcase. One was entitled "Haley's Comet", the title of which was scrawled in sharpie on a piece of paper under the painting. The painting, however, looked nothing like I imagined Haley's Comet to look and actually more resembled the dining counter at a local Burger Box, complete with French fries, milkshakes, free apples and a couple of elderly customers with expanding signs of dementia. Another was called "The Proposal" but appeared to depict a wrecking yard checkers game between two out-of-shape young boys. A third was called "The Cashew" and showed a Joe Montana look-alike sitting on the toilet with a look of sheer terror etched on his face as he confronted some unseen growing crisis in front of him.

The artwork was eclectic and so was the carpet, a fluffy, maroon shag with little critters crawling around in it. My apartment sported a boring brown flat carpet, clean with no hiding places or anything. I probably didn't like the idea of tiny living animals infesting a carpet but I would have liked to at least been presented the option. The furniture was pretty much Goodwill quality, with tears and stains and springs and mold in evidence. On the shelves of the bookcase were dozens of small framed photos, with Tara in a bikini, Tara in a cap and gown, Tara on skis, Tara with friends and many of, I suppose, Tara's parents and siblings. There were probably thirty or forty fishhooks stuck on a wall by the kitchen and what appeared to be fully functioning human intestines dangling from one of them.

"I was hoping to get your help with something," I began, and I noticed as she visibly tensed up, as if expecting a pressurized sales pitch or something worse. "I've been trying to develop a chemical…."

"Are you a scientist?" she interrupted, a little abruptly.

"Why yes, yes I am. I am a scientist and I am trying to develop a chemical to fulfill a need in the marketplace and I would like to get your involvement in the testing phase. It won't hurt, won't be unpleasant in any way. So are you up for a little adventure?"

"I might be up for a little adventure…depends on the depth and the hazard of the adventure."

I sighed. "OK, well I've developed an ointment. Not sure if it's topical or to be ingested but I was hoping that you would try it both ways. Then I want to study you for a couple of hours to gauge its effectiveness."

"What's it for?"

I swallowed hard. "I've been trying to come up with a substance to make loose women or 'whores' appear wholesome and 'nice' in the eyes of a normal male subject. I'm not saying you're loose or anything, but I have noticed that you get a lot of male visitors up here and I assume that there must be sexual activities and diversions going on."

"Oh no, no worries…I'm definitely loose. I wouldn't call myself a whore but I do have lots of men. Men are what I do and there is no shame and no bartering. I love men and especially their things." Tara was opening up in a very forthright manner that I could not help but respect.

"Would you try the ointment and allow me to monitor you for the next couple of hours?"

"Why not? I got a couple of hours to kill. Lay it on me, Taylor."

"I'm not Taylor but that's great!" I was carrying the concoction in my pants pocket in a fogged medicine vial that had previously housed Darvocet. I fished it out and instructed Tara to rub it on her face, her neck, her breasts and her belly, which she did with apparent relish. I then had her spoon the remainder into a coffee cup, add water, nutmeg and baking soda, mix spiritedly and drink. She made a weird little face when she swallowed but I don't think she disliked it too terribly much.

"How do you feel?" I asked expectantly.

"Um, maybe a little woozy – I don't really know yet. It might be too early to say."

"OK". I settled in to begin monitoring Tara and she laid herself down on the couch with a stuffed animal and a Brandy Alexander. I did not see a television anywhere in the apartment so I turned on the dusty clock radio that she kept on an end table to an easy listening station and adjusted the volume down to a very soft and soothing level. Sheena Easton was singing a song of hope, affection, the American way, contemplation and the rigors of straining.

"Mmmm," Tara murmured quietly. "That's really nice."

In the span of just a few minutes, Tara had grown drowsy and seemed so relaxed that I thought she might fall asleep. The stuffed animal fell to the floor and her eyelids began fluttering a little bit. There was a muted snore that began at the very recesses of her esophagus and escaped through her half-opened mouth and mostly unobstructed nose.

"Tara, don't fall asleep."

"I'm not, I'm not," she mumbled and turned her prone body over to face away from me.

Then it happened and I mean it happened with a vengeance. Gas began to spew out of her ass like the dickens and I'm not exaggerating. The foulest smelling odor I can ever remember coming from a human began to fill the room at an alarming rate. Initially, it came in silence but soon it was accompanied by the inevitable sound effects and if it weren't so vile, it would have been comical. It went from little firecracker bursts to these gigantic bombastic sonic booms that seemed to rattle the walls of the tiny apartment. Soon, these explosions began to sound wet and that was obviously more than a guy like me could be expected to handle. I pulled my shirt up over my mouth and nose and hurried for the door. I looked back over my shoulder at Tara; I could see that she was breathing – which was good – and her emissions had become staccato machine bursts, the force of which were actually causing her pants jump about involuntarily. I turned and rushed out her front door, closed it tightly behind me and sprinted down the stairs to my own apartment.

Once inside, I washed my face and hands scrupulously, took off my clothes and put them outside on my back patio to air out. Then I sat cross-legged on my dull brown carpet – naked -- and reflected on the evening's strange events. At first, it seemed as if my experiment had been a miserable failure, a waste of time and resource. Basically, it appeared that all I had accomplished was possibly poisoning a whore and stinking up a building, maybe permanently. Had it made Tara seem wholesome and pure? No, in fact it had caused me to see her in animal terms with little or no control over her bodily functions and the most heinous smelling gas the world had ever known. I could only imagine what went on in the apartment in the minutes and hours after my departure. Things likely got progressively worse and the actual cost of cleanup might have run into the thousands of dollars.

But the more I considered it, the more I realized that I might be on to something. Sure, my invention did not make Tara seem desirable – not in the least. But my invention had enabled me to see her from the perspective of the Devil and had allowed me to gauge the evil that spilled from her ass that cool fall evening in Texas. That funk was obviously curled up inside of her all along, hiding and allowing her to mask her true being with off-brand perfumes, Dollar General bath lotions and African-American hair gel.

I was badly shaken by the harrowing experience with Tara – I really was. Thus, I ended my quest to invent a lotion or spray that made loose women seem pure when applied in proper doses. Tara did not die but we never really spoke again, save for a brief and awkward exchange at the complex laundry room when she was using a rented shovel to fish her clothing from one of the bounding dryers. She moved away not long afterwards. I remember it well because there were about ten or eleven dudes helping with the move and several more that seemed to be lending at least moral support. I seriously think that one of those lending moral support was Frank Stallone and I believe that I could prove it, if it became necessary.

Not long after, an enthusiastic young couple with a baby moved in and they seemed nice enough. However, I could never look at them square without realizing how much they reminded me of the vileness of Tara's undesirable innards. They were living amongst all that filth and I could never shake the feeling. And the unfinished business with my potential discovery has haunted me through the years; I just *know* I could have changed the world, given the proper set of ingredients and a willing test subject with more acceptable dietary habits than my original test subject. Maybe it wouldn't have been "shooting fish in a barrel" but it certainly would have been a huge turn-on for millions.

#8

Storm Chasing With Impunity

FOR AS LONG AS I can remember, I have been intrigued by weather and by the people who earn their livings forecasting the weather. I would never desire to be one of those people in front of the camera, reading and smiling like a goof; I would love to be behind the scenes, analyzing computer data, gauging bar graphs and codes, timing out fronts and storms and whatnot. I think I find weather so interesting because of its lack of predictability, its moody resilience. I've always loved the Weather Channel and have found myself watching for stretches of several hours at a time. I actually had the idea for the Weather Channel first but, unfortunately, never freaking acted on it. By the time I got a squad of hungry lawyers involved, it was too little and far too late.

My buddy Nicky was also a "Weather Nut" and would often come over to my apartment to "ride out" bad storms, or to simply watch the Weather Channel while getting drunk on a concoction alcohol, fruit, grummets and clams. His favorite weather events were tornados, while mine were cloud-to-ground lightning strikes. We both had a thing for bad weather and were always dismayed during Texas summers when there might be 30-60 straight days with nothing but sun – no storms, no rain, nothing! Things always got interesting in spring, however. That's when Texas weather always tends to get its dander up and display its ornery, cantankerous side. It never really gets too bad in the Dallas area but up in the panhandle, oh momma! Up there, bad weather takes hold and makes its living the easy way, if you catch my drift.

Nicky and I used to always dream of how cool it would be to see the really, really nasty stuff up close and personal. He wanted to experience a tornado, to challenge the vortex and deflect the roar with siding. I wanted to harness the energy from a lightning bolt and somehow physically and mentally benefit from its raw, stupendous power and courage. I don't remember the exact conversation but I do know that we came to an agreement of sorts to become storm chasers for a couple of weeks during early May. He would videotape and I would document with the written word and our hope was to develop a movie or documentary – way before the movie "Twister" ever saw the light of day – that would educate the masses on the fury of nature and our predictable helplessness in its path.

We met on a Saturday morning at an Arlington Jack-In The-Box because Nicky wanted to leave his car there to be used by a girl that worked there. I think the girl was only around 16 and Nicky was 27, which was weird but I looked the other way, as usual. We loaded his things into my car – suitcase, tiny bale of hay, air horn, umbrella, cooler and trombone – and we then set off for the Texas Panhandle. We didn't actually have an *exact* destination; we were just going to travel up Hwy 287 toward the names of the towns we always heard on the news in relation to dangerous weather – Amarillo, Childress, Borger, Canyon, Dumas, Pampa, Dalhart, Cactus. Any of these towns or any of a myriad of smaller communities had the potential to bestow upon us the weather event we were so desperately seeking.

We drove out Highway 287 through Fort Worth and then into sheer nothingness for many miles until reaching the swirling metropolis of Wichita Falls. We stopped there to eat at a Golden Corral Buffet and ate nothing but dessert, which cracked up a few of the waitresses and several of the elderly patrons. We pissed, washed our hands and grabbed a few handfuls of candy corn and M&Ms for the road. On the way out, Nicky and I talked to the manager about bad weather and such. He explained to us how Wichita Falls had a history of dangerous tornado events and Nicky began to become visibly excited, in more ways than one.

"Tornados here? For real?" Nicky was jumping up and down with semi-restrained glee. "When? What happened? What the hell happened?"

The manager was a tall, slender, white middle-aged fellow and his nametag said "Doug". He possessed a salt-n-pepper hair color that screamed "experience" and he was more than a little amused by Nicky's enthusiasm for the subject, smiling patronizingly and shaking his head patiently.

"We get 'em most every year. The last really bad one was back in '79. Took out most of the mall, a couple of strip centers and a Captain D's. That one killed a whole bunch of people. We had another pretty bad one 'bout ten years ago – didn't kill any people but caused a ton of damage and killed twenty or thirty pets and rabbits. That one was scary because it was so big – probably a mile wide."

I was solemn at the mention of death but Nicky was letting out a guttural moan – a moan of excitement, anticipation or both I'm guessing. It was odd: The guy was really pretty normal except when it came to weather and tornados; then he transformed into some kind of damn pervert or something.

"Something wrong with your boy here?" Doug was addressing me and nodded over at the enraptured, trembling, and now gyrating Nicky.

"No, no…he just really loves to talk about weather. He wants to become a meteorologist one day. We're actually just passing through here heading to the panhandle to do some real storm chasing."

"Oh! You're a couple of those crazies. We get 'em through here all the time, headin' out to risk their lives to see stuff they can see on television. What's wrong with ya'll? Don't ya'll have any good sense?"

Doug's harsh tone shocked Nicky back to a form of reality. "Good sense? Can you not comprehend the importance of what we're doing? We are going out there to *save lives*! Don't you get that?" Nicky hesitated, staring at Doug's face. There was an uncomfortable silence and then I noticed what Nicky had evidently noticed: A moderately sized white clump was peeking precariously from Doug's left nostril, threatening, it seemed, to leap out of there with extreme gusto.

"What? What is it? What are you looking at, boy?" Just as Doug was really going to light us up, the white clump tumbled from his nostril and crash-landed on the checkout counter below, actually bouncing a couple of times before settling in front of us. Doug stared at it, Nicky stared at it, and I stared at it. Yep, it was caked coke -- no doubt about it.

Doug reached out and deftly swept the clump back toward him onto the floor behind the counter. I was willing to forgive and forget but Nicky was not the forgiving type.

"You're calling us a couple of crazies? Dude, you're the crazy one, snorting that coke and shit. What the fuck is wrong with you? Do you have any idea what that shit does to your brain?" Nicky paused and studied Doug, who had bowed his head and closed his eyes. "You better pray, you fucker. I watched that stuff kill my Uncle Ahmad…and I don't want to lose you, too."

Stunned, Doug looked up, eyes wide and mouth open. Then he began to cry. He came from back behind the counter, walked up to my friend and embraced him. Nicky hugged him back and I believe they both were crying pretty damn gravely. Their embrace lasted several minutes and it looked as if it was starting to degenerate into caressing and pumping when Nicky gently pulled back. Doug wiped tears from his face, smiling sweetly, and then reached out and wiped away Nicky's.

"You're not gonna lose me. I'm gonna be just fine, thanks to you. You know, sometimes things get so boring up here in Wichita Falls that I find myself searching for a way out. I guess that's what coke was for me – a way out. But you've shown me that I'm special, that I matter. I know that you'll always be on my side and that gives me the confidence to use what I have, to be myself. With you on my team, I know that there's nothing I can't do. You've helped me to discover what lies deep within my heart and soul. You've helped me discover *me*."

"Whatever, dude." Nicky patted me on the back. "Let's get outta here before this guy pulls down his pants." With that, we made for the front door, pausing only momentarily to examine a large spider web behind several trend-setting gumball machines.

We went outside to my car and I slipped behind the wheel while Nicky jumped into the passenger seat.

"Do you believe that guy?" Nicky was shaking his head in amazement or something comparable.

"Nicky, you pretty much led him on, you know? You made him think he had a chance."

"What a dick!" I didn't know if Nicky was referring to me or to Doug and I didn't get the opportunity to inquire, as Nicky pulled a straw hat out of nowhere and placed it over his face, dozing off almost immediately. I sped up Highway 287, exceeding the speed limit by anywhere from 12 to 25 miles per hour but never really worrying too much about it. I watched as the signs kept announcing our approach to Amarillo – 180 miles, 145 miles, 108 miles, 87 miles, 59 miles – 46 miles – but I somehow knew that Amarillo was not our best destination. No, for the kind of weather event we were seeking, there was likely only one town that would do.

Plainview was not a tiny town; in fact, by Texas Panhandle standards, it was very large indeed, boasting over 20,000 permanent residents and another 300-400 who wintered there regularly. It was home to a decent-sized college (Wayland Baptist, which was known for basketball and for the ladies) and one of the first, if not the first, Hilton Hotel. Plainview was also famous for repeated harsh weather events such as tornados, lightning strikes, freak snowstorms, and even meteor impacts. For lovers of bad weather, Hawaiian shirts and feces-covered splendor, there could be no better place than Plainview, Texas in the early spring.

With a disgusting paper map and some fancy maneuvering, I found my way to Highway 27, which supposedly led to the desired destination. This highway was BAD, much of it dusty, poorly marked and full of holes and, in some cases, small canyons. The shaking and racket of the car roused Nicky from his self-imposed slumber, which had lasted a few hours by this point.

"Change of plans, Nick. We're not going to Amarillo."

"OK...." He looked over at me drowsily.

"I've decided that we're going to Plainview."

"Plainview, Plainview....I know that name....Wayland Baptist, right?"

"Yep. Wayland Baptist, the first Hilton Hotel and a diner called 'Gloria's' that only serves stuff that they kill themselves."

"Sign me up! Sounds weighty!" Nicky was enthused and his enthusiasm permeated throughout the car and even into the roadside wilderness, where jackrabbits and armadillos seemed to serenade each other with Sinatra songs, skillfully stepping about to the beat with class.

Before too long, we were pulling into the town of Plainview. This place was literally in the middle of nowhere, vast miles of wasteland surrounding and essentially imprisoning the quaint community. Most of the downtown area appeared old and dilapidated, with numerous buildings boarded shut and some of the buildings that *were* functional proving to be nothing more than an embarrassment to the senses. A few parts of the business district appeared either rebuilt or modern; there was a vibrant Laundromat, a colorful insurance company, a florescent-by-nature trading post and an energetic incense shop. We passed by Gloria's, its huge sign out front boasting that they only served what they themselves killed. Looking closely between buildings, we could see the actual slaughterhouse in the back and the outside walls even looked senselessly bloody. I wondered if they killed their prey humanely and if the menu included raw carcasses – or if everything had to be at least somewhat prepared with heat.

"Let's go find Wayland Baptist!" I think Nicky must have been eager to see something more feminine.

"Why don't we find a place to stay first," I replied, always managing to be the practical one in most any group and especially this one.

"Yeah, alright. I *could* use a shower. I'm pretty funky over here...got little things crawlin' around in my pubes."

"That's *way* more than I needed to hear, you moron."

We found a little hotel called "Dena's" and it looked nice enough, with handsome landscaping, paved and striped parking lots and lighted signs without burned-out bulbs. We purchased a one-week rental, which included two beds, local television, a miniature fridge and coupons for Gloria's on the wood-paneled nightstand. I suspected that Gloria and Dena might be related but when I inquired about this at the front desk later that evening, I was sternly rebuffed and nearly arrested. I decided to drop the subject for the time being.

Darkness was descending on Plainview. There was no Weather Channel on the television supplied by Dena's, so we began searching for local news to find out what was happening with the weather. There was but one local televised newscast and the anchor looked like Mr. Kotter from the TV show, only without one of his eyes. He didn't wear a patch, either; he apparently reveled in displaying the mass of red corpuscles, twisted veins and juicy matter in the spot where his right eye should have been. When "Kotter" finally got to the local weather, it did not seem promising for Nicky and me: Partly cloudy skies, 20% chance of rain with nothing severe expected. This was a downer but we still had plenty of time; in the meantime, Nicky wanted to cruise Wayland Baptist and see what was what out there. I gave him the car keys, wished him more power and crawled into the semi-comfortable bed for what I hoped would be a decent night's sleep.

I was awakened by the sounds of Nicky pawing, sniffing and licking this bird that he had pulled from the Wayland Baptist campus or maybe some other fertile spot. Our beds were a few feet apart but it seemed like the two of them were right on top of me – and then they were. Nicky lifted the girl up and dropped her clumsily onto my bed, with him following up right behind, so to speak. There was an intense odor of alcohol prevalent as they wrestled each other and unintentionally wrestled me. I could not really see the girl but I could tell she was pretty small and when a boob smashed into my face, I knew that her endowment was rotund. I vocalized my protestations but they were falling on truly deaf ears.

It wasn't long before I found myself flat on my back, the girl lying sideways across my bed with the back of her head on my stomach, and Nicky mounting her and commencing drilling. I believe that she had *just* figured out that there was another guy in the bed and she didn't seem too adverse to the situation. I rebuffed her somewhat amorous advance because it was just too alternative and I somehow managed to fall asleep, probably made easier by the symphonic rocking of Nicky's thrusts. This was, maybe without question, the strangest night of sleep I had ever accomplished -- it really was. And when I awoke the following morning, I was alone; both Nicky and the girl had split and left behind just a few signs that they had actually been there. On my bed I noticed a bit of Nicky's back hair, several greasy chicken fingers, what looked like a female's painted toenail, an owner's manual for to a '86 Pontiac Fiero and some outdated heartworm medication in a prematurely crumpled tube.

Curious about the weather, I switched on the television and there was that same "Kotter" guy from the night before, now working the morning shift. Maybe he worked all the shifts; maybe he lived at the television station and tore the toenails from the feet of girls during late night trysts. Maybe he bathed in lumpy cream gravy and used copper-plated fishing rods for something unorthodox. He delivered the local news in his predictable deadpan: Local street paving project behind schedule; police arrest two for vandalism and streaking; mayor says town needs help with a planting scenario. Then Kotter got to the weather portion of the show and it seemed like very good news indeed: Severe thunderstorm warning for the area tonight and tomorrow -- possible hail and tornado activity. Yes!!!

It was imperative that I find Nicky to form our relative plan of action. I went out to the parking lot and my car was nowhere to be seen and I could only assume that Nicky had used it to drive the girl home or somewhere equivalent. I went back into the hotel room and picked up the phone to beep him – two minutes later, I got a call back from the actor Jim Nabors and it was obvious that I had the wrong beeper number. Jim Nabors was nice, though, and patiently answered my questions about Gomer Pyle, Burt Reynolds, Placido Domingo, Eskimo Pies and Cher. We hung up but not before making plans to see each other the next time he came to Dallas.

I waited in the room for Nicky's return. An hour…two hours… four hours…six hours. It became obvious that Nicky's return was not imminent. I briefly considered contacting local authorities out of concern for his safety but decided that would expose me to a level of scrutiny for which I was not prepared. Day turned to night and I got jittery as I considered the possible scenarios. I guessed that it was conceivable that Nicky had stolen my car and ran off somewhere with the Wayland Baptist girl. He may have encountered some type of foul play though that did not seem too likely in Plainview, Texas. He could have just lost track of the time while playing miniature golf or whittling. He may have been involved in some kind of dental office tragedy or harpoon training. This was all disconcerting, to say the least. Part of my soul cried like a baby while another part giggled from the unexpected and smoking insanity.

Over the course of the next rainy two days, I sat in that hotel room waiting and watching the local television newscasts as Kotter reported on a Wayland Baptist coed that had not been seen or heard from in some 53 or 54 hours. I was scared – I really was. Finally, I determined that I had waited long enough and the time had arrived for me to run away from this thing and to get as far away as possible without calling undue attention to myself. I checked out of the hotel, walked half a mile to the downtown bus station and hopped a Greyhound bus for home.

The bus ride back to the Dallas area was an excruciating 22 hour ordeal, complete with 15 stops, a statuesque driver, a crying baby and three vomiting elderly people who made disgraceful hacking noises during the act. Our bus also hit a cat on the highway between Wichita Falls and Fort Worth. Not only did the driver hit the cat but he braked and slowed the bus to a stop (in the middle of the highway), backed up and ran the cat over a couple of additional times, I guess to humanely put it out of its misery. I'd always figured that cats were too smart and too quick to get hit by vehicles, especially buses, but our driver proved me wrong on this occasion. It was a miserable trip and I was wracked with guilt over the abandonment of my friend and the failure of my stated mission. I had not experienced a tornado and I saw zero cloud-to-ground lightning strikes. It rained a bit and I heard a few rumbles of thunder but the weather was nothing at all out of the ordinary. Most of a week had been completely wasted and this was a week from my life that was lost forever. Forever.

About three weeks after my return home, I heard from some friends that Nicky was alive and had actually moved to San Francisco and found work as a part-time radio talk show host. He had married a girl named Cicily after a whirlwind week-long romance and they moved to Northern California to escape any prospect of severe weather. I never knew if Cicily was the same girl he had brought back to the hotel room that night but I did hear that she owned far too many wool sweaters and had written an encrypted program for the military's computer system. Nicky eventually lost his radio job because of prolonged belching on the air and discovered a new career in engorged zoology, rising to the top of the ranks in the field with a prowess previously unknown to the human race. He shaved his head before it was fashionable and started taking mud baths with barely legal teenagers in the heart of the city on alternating Wednesdays and Saturdays in the early evenings.

Losing my weather buddy was tremendously disappointing. There were many more Texas towns to explore during weather events – Big Stinking Creek, Noodle and Pringle were high on my list. Every time the weather turned a tad dicey, I couldn't help but recall Nicky's favorite quotation, delivered by, of all people, General George Custer:

"After spending years warring against witless savages throughout this great land, it is always comforting to know that I can return home… home to a place where I can dress up frilly and drape myself in lace without the prospect of condemnation or unwarranted scrutiny – home to a place where my diet is my own and the pot is always calling the kettle something rude."

#9

Something Great, Something Borrowed

MY BRUSHES WITH CELEBRITY have been few and far between and my brushes with true greatness even more rare. These two elements – celebrity and true greatness – only very seldom intersect within a single individual, as far as I can tell. Dylan, Eleonor Bron, Fitzgerald, Fat Joe, Gretzky, Hans Memling, Einstein, Buster Keaton, Stephen Butler Leacock, Sissy Farenthold and Flying Red Bastein are just about the only ones that come immediately to mind. In my opinion, celebrities are normally not truly great – usually just lucky – and truly great individuals are likely to be completely unknown to the masses -- such is the way of this world.

I've experienced only a few notable encounters with celebrity-types and many of these were notably under-whelming. I shook both hands with Elton John. I briefly spoke on the phone with Jim Nabors. I actually had a longer phone conversation with Jack Klugman. A college friend of mine who was an entertainment reporter for the school newspaper had somehow acquired Jack Klugman's home phone number and convinced me that I needed to call him up and ask him to reveal Quincy's first name. Mr. Klugman was none too pleased to be hearing from the likes of me and lectured me on responsibility and privacy issues. He also told me that Quincy's first name was Theo; people never believe me when I tell them that Quincy's first name was Theo. I guess I should have taken the opportunity to ask him about his character's fondness of knives in "Twelve Angry Men" but I evidently choked away the opportunity.

On a trip to Vegas, I ended up at the Imperial Palace playing blackjack at a $10 table with the guy who played Mannix on television. It was just me, him and the faux Cuban dealer -- I was very young and really didn't know what I was doing. Mannix shot me a couple of questioning looks when I made some dumb plays and then began grunting audibly with disdain at the way in which I continued to play the game. Strangely, however, I was winning money and he was losing money – lots of money. I estimate that he lost probably $300 or $500 during my thirty minutes or so at the table and ultimately stormed off in a bit of a rage. I think I ended up winning $90, maybe a little bit more.

I very nearly received head from Marilu Henner in a clump of bushes behind a Piggly Wiggly. I believe she was doing some kind of appearance at the location and I needed some potted meat, seltzer and a loaf of bread. I might have been a little intoxicated and wandered into what I thought was the men's restroom; turned out, it was the lady's restroom and I walked in on Marilu Henner while she was doing her private business. She was initially shocked but then we sort of hit it off. She confided in me that Judd Hirsch was "reliable" and Tony Danza was "kinda squirrelly". One thing led to another and I probably proposed a scenario that would take us to the bushes out in back of the store. I remember distinctly that she wholeheartedly agreed, provided that I could guess her middle name and date of birth. After careful consideration, I guessed "Susan" and 7/20/55. Marilu smiled impishly and told me that she was sincerely sorry but I was wrong, though I had been close. Curses!

I shared a joke about mousetraps with Emmitt Smith, placed my hand admiringly on the bicep of Herschel Walker and picked up a big bag of yellow pills dropped by Johnny Cash in an airport terminal. I put O.J. Simpson in a friendly headlock and hit a series of shags with Maureen Starkey and one member of Sister Sledge. On a Thursday in 1987, I stopped to help a stranded motorist along Interstate 30. The stranded motorist was obviously Michelle Phillips from the Mamas and the Papas – it just had to be -- though she did not say it in so many words. I said "hello" and popped her hood to take a look at the motor and whatnot. I'm no mechanic but I tried fiddling with battery cables, transmission wiring, engine piping and rotary muzzles. I told her to try to start the car again, but it only made a whirring and then a series of clicking sounds. I checked water levels, bolt stability and belts and hoses and the car still refused to start.

Unable to get her car running, I offered to take Michelle Phillips to the nearest service station so that she could obtain more competent, experienced assistance. She gratefully accepted and lamented the fact that she had been broken down for nearly an hour and that I was the only person who had stopped to help. Watching out for traffic, I helped her from her car and walked her up to my car that was parked in front, opened the passenger side door and aided her as she slid in. Michelle was a beauty – graceful and feminine – and I was enjoying the view intently. I walked around behind my car to the driver's side, hopped in, started the car and merged carefully into traffic. It was only about two miles to the next exit and there stood a Texaco station, strong, tall and even menacing.

"Are you Michelle Phillips? You are, aren't you?"

"I get that a lot," she replied coyly. "You are a *very* nice guy. And cute… and such a gentleman!"

"I like to help people, especially beautiful women. I'm so sorry your car conked out on you."

"Eh…it's a piece of shit. It was just a matter of time. How can I…" She hesitated, obviously uncertain.

"How can you what?"

"How can I thank you for your kindness? There is no telling how long I would have sat there if you hadn't stopped. I'm sure you have places to be yet you spent your valuable time helping me."

"Hmmm…how can you thank me? That's a bit of a loaded question, don't you think?" We both kind of chuckled nervously.

Then she turned deadly serious. "I would be happy to fiddle with you in some way – foolishly – for your kindness. I would really be happy to."

I, too, became serious. "As tempting as that offer is, I don't need you to do that. I'm just really glad I was able to help."

We pulled up to the front door of the station. Michelle looked over at me with a gorgeous, broad smile. "Well, I'm betting you can find me if you change your mind, right?" Then she leaned over in the seat and kissed me on the cheek. "Bye!" she said and, grabbing her purse, popped out of the car and walked through the front door of the establishment, pausing briefly to glance back over her shoulder at me. I considered hanging out there for a bit to make sure she found the help she needed; I thought the better of it because I was starting to feel nauseous and gassy and didn't want someone who might have been Michelle Phillips to see me in that condition.

In terms of celebrities, the other ones whose paths I've crossed through the years have been Ray Wylie Hubbard, Dan Rather, Nancy Lieberman, Paul Harvey, Ramon Martinez, Anson Williams, Sergeant Shriver and Kathy Ireland. I did witness the singer Meatloaf send back a sandwich at a downtown deli, claiming that the onions "tasted like puppies". As for the truly great, I have known only a few. Most prominent would be a soccer coach who separated the kooks from the credible with a procedure he dubbed "dritterbussing" – he eventually patented the technique. Another great person was the orthopedic surgeon who fixed my blown-out knee with a series of prayers, molded rubber and eerily suggestive rain dances. Still another was a pinball machine technician who had no hands but possessed the ingenuity to wrap his stumps in pickle loaf to soften the blow at least a bit.

Maybe the greatest person I ever ran across was also one of the most obscure. Her name was Kat and she worked as an apprentice to a seamstress in a local shopping center. I met her shortly after I ripped my pants while choking on a hunk of beef at a strip club buffet. I took the pants in for repair and she was most helpful indeed, analyzing the tear in specific terms and suggesting a cohesive solution that would not cost all that much. She passed my pants on to the eighty year-old head seamstress and proceeded to ring up my purchase in no uncertain terms.

"That's $5.41 including the tax, sir. And we'll have it ready by noon tomorrow."

"OK." I gave her a twenty and she provided nearly accurate change with a flourish.

"Thanks for coming in!"

But something about her was troubling to me. "What are you all about?" I asked. "What inhabits that mind of yours?"

"What do you mean?"

I studied her face for a sign, any sign. Kat was around twenty and possibly an albino, with ocean-blue eyes, snow-blonde hair and just a wisp of a blonde moustache above thin, wrinkly lips. She wasn't obese but she certainly wasn't tiny either – maybe thirty pounds on the wrong side of her ideal weight. She was dressed in a "KISS" t-shirt and had holes in her jeans before it was all the rage. Kat was barefoot behind the counter and she appeared to be maybe a women's shoe size 12 – goddamn big. But I sensed something special in her essence; she exuded a soothing confidence that was driving me to know more.

"You're working on something, aren't you? You've got something in the works. I can tell."

Kat bit her lower lip. "You're very perceptive."

"What is it? What's going on? You can tell me."

"Not here. Come outside with me." Kat took me by the hand and led me out the front door onto a sidewalk littered with cigarette butts and barely digested hoagies.

Kat released my hand and dug into her pants pocket, fishing out a wrinkled bit of notebook paper with scribbling and seeming gibberish.

"Alright." She manufactured the kind of sigh that you might hear from a travel agent. "I'm not through testing this yet but I think I have hit on a formula to synthesize food – all types of food – for about three cents on the dollar. I can do meat, vegetables, fruits, bread – even root beer floats -- only more healthy and nutritious. And the beauty is that the supply can be limitless because at its core, my formula utilizes salt water, sand and litter."

Now she was the one studying my face and I must say that I was totally blown away, awestruck. I had always fancied myself as an inventor of stuff and this albino girl had come up with an idea that was difficult for me to take in. I finally managed a hoarse "Wow."

"Yeah, pretty big, huh?" She was gazing at her little scrap of paper. Suddenly, she looked back up at me. "Do you want to see this?"

Indeed I did. I held out my hand and she gave me the formula. It did not make a lot of sense to me and I don't remember all of it but I do remember seeing "$Y = 648R2xZL95904+XMOP377$." There was much more to it than that but for whatever reason, that part of the formula stuck in my head and the remainder escaped. I carefully handed it back to her, my hand trembling a bit.

"You know, Kat…this would be the most important invention in the history of mankind. You would totally erase the world's hunger problem and save millions of lives. You would alleviate suffering and I imagine this would go a long way toward curing America's obesity epidemic. I don't know what to say, I really don't."

"Say that you'll help me."

"What could *I* do?"

"Right now, this is just a theory, a hypothesis. I need someone to help me make this happen. I need a go-getter. I need you."

"Kat, you don't even know me. I'm the type of guy that tends to run from things. I submerge my troubles in raw honey and will often go days between baths or showers. I don't like rodeos and I don't appreciate the plight of the unenlightened. And due to a couple of my afflictions, I'm probably the last person you need helping you ramrod your idea. I really am a mess and you deserve something better. You *require* something better."

"But I don't *desire* something better…"

"Kat, no way this could work. You know it and I know it. But I sincerely hope that you make a go of it. I hope you make it happen."

"Thanks." Kat became subdued. "That means a lot. I'll keep you posted."

Kat wasn't there when I picked up my pants the following day. The old seamstress said that she had a "fervent preoccupation due to some unrelated mental stress". I think this meant that she had resigned to follow some higher calling, though there was no way to know for sure. I soon saw a couple of snippets about Kat in newspapers and on local news. Her idea was noble but, according to reports, she had evidently encountered roadblocks and resistance. The mega food companies and restaurant chains hated her and used their influences to cause her misery and shame. The U.S. Department of Agriculture denounced her as a "fraud", a "scammer" and a "dirty albino" and encouraged citizens to shun her in public and to egg her house. I'm certain that Kat was unprepared for this sort of cruel vitriol and she retreated like frightened foliage.

One cold December morning, Kat called a press conference at a Holiday Inn and wordlessly set fire to the crumpled piece of paper that contained the formula. She walked dejectedly from the podium as the paper burned and the fire crackled. A slovenly man from audience wearing a tank top grabbed an extinguisher from the wall and sprayed like the dickens, killing the fire. Kat never looked back and strode from the room like a sniveling pilgrim, evidently anxious to put the entire ordeal behind her.

A few years later, I happened to catch her obituary in the newspaper, a small blurb that mentioned she was an inventor, an albino and an activist who had suffered from an accidental overdose of swine and red pills. The story listed no family members to speak of and alluded to no particular interests or religion. I was inconsolable at the realization that one of the world's great minds had died the lonely death of a cruel alcoholic vagrant. I went to the funeral, which was held in a tiny white chapel in Balch Springs. There were only 17 people there, including the minister and the old seamstress. Minister Brent hailed Kat for her brave spirit, her undying devotion and her calm demeanor. He asked for those in attendance to stand up and share a memory about Kat. I stood up, intending to pay homage to her brilliance but instead ended up laughing manically like some kind of moron. The old seamstress was NOT happy with me and shushed me not once, not twice, but three times.

#10

Stomach Flu: The Unappetizing Art of a Famished Soul

GOING THROUGH A WEE bit of a crisis at age 30, I decided for some reason to take up painting. Never had painted before, never had been the least bit interested in that form of art. It just seemed like it could provide an applicable outlet for some of the stuff that ailed me and some of the stuff that was biting me in the ass, so to speak. There were no delusions of grandeur, no outrageous expectations; I just thought it might be fun and therapeutic and messy all at the same time.

I didn't have a clue where to begin so I went to a Michael's store and started asking questions. The teenaged help managed to direct me to some brushes and some paints and a pallet and some good, strong paper. A couple of the female bottoms were trying to inspire me in some way but I asserted individual mind control to quell the threat. I decided that abstract art looked easy and would be a good jumping off point; that is, abstract art would cause less disappointment for me than a poorly painted vase or beer can or ranch or clown face.

At home, I rearranged an unused home office into a type of art studio, complete with wall hangings, frilly lace, a futon and smelling salts. I surrounded myself with my favorite books, records, photographs and aromas, hopeful of manufacturing a muse or inspirational mechanism. I never had a real sister but I built one and stuck her in the closet, desperate to receive the kind of sisterly support that I had observed in the families of some of my childhood friends.

When painting day arrived, I was unusually nervous. I stalked around the pallet -- stopping, staring and wondering what Henry Kissinger would do if he were in my shoes. It took a couple of hours for me to even get started and once I did, the going was slow, slow and slower. I used my brush to swipe and slash red paint across and along the middle of the paper and tried to transfer some anguish from my past onto the expectant canvas. Then I applied some black paint and gold paint in sweeping strokes that actually obscured some of the red, but not all of it. It took almost the entire day but I finally managed to finish an abstract painting that I named "Owner of a Substandard Apartment Community". I immediately taped it to the wall in my art studio and I was off the first tee.

I began to crank out about two abstract paintings per day. "Silly Marijuana Bong", "Pennant on the Wall of Strife", "The World According to Crystal Meth", "Preeminent Eye Socket", "Dead Squirrels and Aces", "Pocket Protector Snowball" and "Hammer of George McGovern" all came out perfectly and were dutifully hung on the studio wall. Abstract painting turned out to be more difficult than I imagined but it was also great fun! At the beginning of a work, I had no idea where it would lead but it was as if something or someone looped a leash or chain around my neck and drug me awkwardly to an ultimate final destination. I knew when a work was finished – I just knew it – and the completion of a painting would result in a little miniature tea party for myself and my long-time imaginary friends. Lester, Toronto Terri, Mango Marvin, Phillip and Florence the Bad Kisser had been with me since childhood; it was difficult to imagine my life without them. They had seen me through tough times, celebrated with me during times of plenty and counseled me when I knew not what to do. My five imaginary friends were five of my top ten friends in the world, with Mango Marvin checking in at number one and Florence the Bad Kisser at number four. It was difficult for my human friends to compete with my imaginary friends because my human friends had wills of their own and didn't live to serve and entertain me. No question, I needed my imaginary friends and they were each critical to my personal development and growth patterns.

I concentrated on abstracts for three months or so and was accumulating quite a stimulating gallery but I felt that the time had come to experiment with other styles. After careful consideration, I decided to attempt to paint Mister T. Obviously, he was unavailable for live modeling but I found many photographs and watched quite a lot of his television shows and the Rocky 3 movie a bunch of times. I was able to get Mister T's face tattooed on my brain, emblazoned in my consciousness to such a degree that his was the face of every person I encountered, every person I imagined.

The Mister T project took me a total of four days and I wasn't completely satisfied with the finished product. I couldn't get the hair right and I had difficulty with the bridge of the nose. I also gave him a damn high forehead and his eyes looked like Shelly Long eyes. Reluctantly, I showed some of my human friends and their reactions were predictably mixed. A couple of them said "Ah, cool", one thought I had painted an Egyptian sculptor and another said that my painting reminded him of Truman Capote on an alcohol-driven cocaine binge.

For my next project, I decided to attempt to paint Joe Walsh. I was a fan of Joe Walsh and I made it my highest priority to get it right. Surprisingly, however, the real Joe Walsh has many lines on his face that go up and down and other lines on his face that go side to side. This was impossible for me to capture with any degree of accuracy and I ended up making the lines look like a series of Grand Canyons. I also encountered significant problems with his neck because of some colorful bulging veins that I was unable to depict realistically. Two different people I showed this painting thought I had painted Golda Meir, not Joe Walsh. I was initially a little pissed off but as I examined my work, I had to concede their point.

A painter friend that I know had warned me that painting people was hard – real hard. I began to see his point but I was not ready to give up the hobby. Over the protests of almost everyone, I decided to paint a nude. And I was going to have to paint the nude from imagination only, since I would not have a sitting, posing nude in my studio. After agonizing deliberation, the nude I decided to paint: Olivia Newton-John.

I found eight or nine Olivia Newton-John albums at a flea market and placed them strategically through my studio. I watched "Grease" and "Xanadu" a few times and let my imagination run wild. I figured that the way I could judge my success or failure would be if I became aroused during the creation of the work. If something slopped onto canvas could produce physical arousal, it had to be good…right?

Work on the Olivia Newton-John nude began late on a Thursday night and after a couple of beers. I started with her blonde hair and managed to complete hair, forehead, eyebrows and ears before I decided to call it a night. I had planned to get the eyes completed but I ran into a little trouble – there were significant differences in her eyes on some albums from her eyes on other albums and in the movies. Looked to me like she might have had some eye work done and I prudently shelved the eyes until the following night, determining that waiting was the right thing to do before tackling the eye portion of the project.

When I awoke the next morning, I could not wait to get back to the painting. The eyes from the "Totally Hot" album would be the eyes for my project. I really wish I could say that this came to me in a dream but that night I had dreamt about Vlade Divac, not Olivia. He wanted to run for President of the French Republic but he wasn't a citizen. Despite this, he somehow won the presidency as a write-in candidate and his first order of business was to replace the French currency with pelts of mink. He survived a couple of assassination attempts by Charles Bronson but eventually abdicated his presidency to pursue a relationship with porn star Gloria Leonard.

Anyway, I worked on the eyes for several hours and somehow got them just right. Nose and cheeks went quickly but the mouth slowed the process to the proverbial crawl. Olivia always had a very big smile flashing bright white teeth that were awfully straight except for one on the left side of the bottom row that was inset about 1/16 of an inch and tilted ever so slightly back. It also looked to me like there might be a minor case of gum disease, though I had no way of knowing for sure. I labored on the mouth for the remainder of the day and for almost half of the next day, finally settling on a depiction that looked very inviting indeed! Finished off the face with a cute jutting chin and since it was time to move south, the time had come to move south.

Necks were always tough for me; Adam's Apples and throats are so variable and thickness and tone can be tricky. Olivia's neck was real easy, however, and I flew through it in half an hour or so. Her shoulders also proved to be a relative breeze; she displayed them prominently for most of the late seventies and early eighties and I pretty well knew them by heart. It was obvious that she worked out and her shoulders were definitely the beneficiaries. I sketched in the outline of her torso and worked on her two arms for several hours. Olivia was quite toned and her hands were bigger than I had expected them to be. They weren't what you would call "manly hands" but they were a little less feminine than you would think.

I postponed the breasts and center torso and headed down to the legs and feet. Olivia's legs were outstanding and her feet were pleasantly small, especially when considering the large hands. I sketched in a couple of scars on her knees because I imagined she must have experienced some surgeries here and there along the way. I also gave her a blackened toenail; anyone that works out a lot most likely has a blackened toenail and I was certain that Olivia worked out a lot. So she received a blackened toenail in my painting.

The breasts and vaginal area were looming and, though it was very late, I decided to push onward. I hated to imagine Olivia with an overgrown forest of pubic hair – it just did not seem right. But at the point in time of this depiction, you just knew there had to be *some*. Not much, but at least *some*. So I soaked my brush in black paint and went to town. Yes, black paint because, based on some early pictures of Olivia that I had seen, she was not a natural blonde. Unfortunately, I got too aggressive with the black paint and made things more "lush" than initially planned. It was a deadly serious mishap but I decided that I had no choice but to live with it.

The seriously flat belly took no time and it appeared that all that was left were the breasts. And here I evidently took leave of my senses. It was obvious that Olivia's breasts were small and there was nothing wrong with that. They looked good on her and she wore them well – she really did. However, for whatever reason, I got carried away and before I realized it, I had given her the breasts of Jane Mansfield, with nipples the size of fully-grown earthworms. And, paradoxically, I decided to cover them in tattoos and dangerous looking moles, which made them most unattractive and extremely unappetizing. I did all this and I wasn't even drunk or high or anything; it was like someone or something had commandeered my mind and committed an unthinkable act of evil. I had spent days on this creation and seemed to have lost my mind at the very end of the process.

After a good, long weeping session, I stepped back to analyze my finished work. The breasts were tragic, no doubt about it, but I liked what I saw in other places -- not enough to become aroused, mind you, but parts of her looked realistic and not overly scary. The hair, eyebrows, arms and legs were exceptional. The crotch was problematic, to say the least, but the belly damn near compensated. I wasn't sure if this was good enough to show others and neither were my imaginary friends. They presented legitimate criticism and debated whether this piece was worthy of a public view. In the end, we couldn't find a consensus and I decided to allow a half dollar to make the decision: "Heads" I throw the painting away; "Tails" I show it to some of my friends. The half dollar arbitrarily determined that I should show the painting around.

My painter friend was the first to see it and he winced like he had a daunting case of bleeding bunions.

"I told you that painting people was hard. What's up with those breasts? And how much pubic hair do you think she has? Jeez!"

But several of my other friends actually liked it, or so they said. My friend Brenda said it looked somewhat like the work of Picasso. Bradford said he sensed genius in the making and he was anxious to buy stock in me. Cindy proclaimed it my "masterpiece" and offered to purchase it on the spot for whatever was in her pocket. Dennis was impressed to the point of recommending enshrinement into some kind of art "hall of fame". Bolstered by their apparent enthusiasm, I took the painting to a downtown art dealer that I found in the yellow phone book. He basically stopped me at the front door with prejudice.

"I don't look at unsolicited work," he said tersely and sort of blocked my way with a rope he was dragging around.

"You'll want to see this!" and I proceeded to remove the painting from its sleeve and held it up proudly.

"What the fuck is that?" The cranky art dealer actually sounded frightened.

"I call it 'A Performer's Hey Day' and it took me a really long time to complete."

Enraged, the art dealer pulled a gun on me; this was the first time a gun had ever been pointed at me and I didn't like it at all.

"Get the fuck out of here or I'll waste your ass. And take that piece of shit monstrosity with you. Leave…now!"

Alright…so maybe painting people was too hard for me. I attempted several inanimate objects (a sock, a fax machine, a purse, a can of motor oil) but didn't like the results. Next, I tried animals. I painted a gold fish in a plastic bag, a burro, a bird of prey, a garter snake and an ingenuously disabled cocker spaniel. Nothing leapt off the page. Then I decided to attempt food and I noticed that my results improved dramatically. I painted a bowl of oatmeal with cinnamon that looked good enough to have for breakfast; a tamale wrapped in bacon with smoke wafting from the edges; a coffee-soaked banana covered with bruises; a crab cake smothered in soy sauce and topped with a single birthday candle; and a Great White shark fillet served with tender scallops. Maybe painting food was my specialty! All of my real and imaginary friends simply raved about the food paintings. Even my painter friend said he liked them, that they displayed a great deal of promise. I didn't dare ask the art dealer downtown but I was encouraged enough by the response to arrange a public showing of my stuff.

I rented out a Holiday Inn conference room, put a small advertisement in the newspaper and called the event "Stomach Flu: The Unappetizing Art of a Famished Soul". In all, I think I hung around 35 paintings of different foods – some already digested – for view and review by interested art lovers and potential art buyers. Was I disappointed that only some human friends, imaginary friends, a cocktail waitress and Gaylord Perry showed up? Of course I was. I had hoped that the event would generate some interest and buzz concerning my work. But when Gaylord Perry offered to buy all of my paintings for his mother-in-law's new house, I felt an intense swell of vindication. Of course I was forced to turn down his generous offer of ten bucks per painting in the name of artistic integrity – but it was damn cool that he offered.

I don't know if I actually lost interest in painting but I do know that at some point I just stopped. Maybe it was time constraints, maybe it was El Nino…I'm really not sure. I went through a poem-writing phase and for a number of months, I was cranking out three poems a day, most of them limericks with a few sonnets mixed in for good measure. Then I became interested in magic and spent dozens of hours honing my skills in illusion and card tricks. This gave way to a short-term obsession with the occult that nearly got me beat up and that transitioned into the hobby of gardening, which proved relaxing, physically challenging and slightly effeminate.

I've only picked up a paintbrush a couple of times during the ensuing years, once due to a stressful situation involving a broken pallet and another time when I butchered the trimming of my two eyebrows. These paintings, variably abstract, served to calm me down better than any drug ever could. Painting will always hold a special place in my heart and when I find myself missing it, I try to experience the whole wide world in the best possible way.

#11

Manson-Face and a Doctor's Science

A WOMAN I KNEW from work several years ago was forced to quit after she received a grim diagnosis of "Manson-Face". Evidently, this was a little-known affliction that caused a person's face to become paralyzed or "freeze" into a Charles Manson-like glare for hours on end. At the time, there was no known cure for "Manson-Face" and the disease made it nearly impossible for someone to function effectively in our society. She did not want to quit but her illness frightened our customers and resulted in a loss of volume, which was unacceptable to our senior management staff and their beneficiaries. It was a case of either quit or face termination; Priscilla had her pride and decided to step down voluntarily. I felt terrible about her situation and was fiercely determined to find some way to help with her predicament.

It was a tragic thing for anyone to endure but especially for such a pretty woman. Without Manson-Face, Priscilla was very nice looking, a real head-turner. I think she was a Hispanic/Caucasian mix with light brown hair to her shoulders in the back, big brown eyes and a slim, toned build. Priscilla had the look of an athlete, maybe a soccer player or volleyballer. But when Manson-Face broke out (which seemed to happen nearly every day), she became a hideous, slobbering monster. She couldn't speak; thus, she communicated with a pattern of grunts, groans and moans, often wildly waving hands and arms 'round to make a point. She had to wear a bib on her chest to catch the constant flow of saliva from the mouth and mucous from the nose and what the bib didn't catch would stain her clothing or pool onto the floor in front of her. It was just impossible for her to care for herself during an outbreak of Manson-Face and it seemed improbable that anyone would voluntarily hang out to help.

When Priscilla entered my office on that warm summer morning to hand in her resignation letter, she was looking great – bright, cheery, a ray of frickin' sunshine. She was handling it so much better than I was and this made me feel even worse about the unfortunate situation.

"Priscilla, I feel so bad about all of this. I really wish there was another way."

"It's gonna be OK. My mother always told me that everything happens for a reason. There's a bigger plan for me and I'm just waiting to see what it is."

"What are you going to do now?"

"Well, I was thinking about going back to school. I only lack about 15 hours to get my associates, so I may do that. And my brother told me that there might be an opening at his work in the eastside mortuary. So we'll see."

"What are you going to do about your Manson-Face?"

"What *can* I do? Just deal with it, I guess…like I always have."

"Listen, I know this doctor…well, he's sort of a doctor…"

"Sort of a doctor?" she interrupted, staring at me incredulously.

"OK, let me back up. He doesn't have a doctorate but he practices what you might call alternative medicine. He takes on cases that are strange or unheard of. He's really, really good. There was a story about him in the Observer. Anyway, I can talk to him about your case and hook ya'll up if you like."

Priscilla stared at her feet for a long time, and then looked up at me. "Would you go with me? I'll agree to see him if you'll go with me."

"Sure I will. I'll talk to him tonight and I'll call you tomorrow. Is that cool?"

"It is." She stood to leave and reached out to shake my hand. I grasped her hand and we shook for an uncomfortably long period of time. She eventually released and turned to head for my office door. Then she looked back over her shoulder. "I've loved working here. You're a really great boss. I'm going to miss everybody very much. It's just so sad."

I began to tear up and I was not ashamed of it. "We're gonna miss *you*. Thanks for all of your service. You've been a model employee." I had to find a way to help this girl.

That very night, I called Dr. Willie. He had not technically earned a doctorate but insisted that he be called "Doctor" anyway. He was brilliant, maybe the smartest person I have ever known. He was the type that could have accomplished anything in life that he set his mind to – no question about it. And he chose to practice "back room" medicine, challenging diseases and abnormalities that traditional medicine did not have the time for. He had an innate compassion for those that had been cruelly stricken by the rare oddities and had devoted his life to helping them. Of course, he also benefited from the fact that many of his patients were willing to spend whatever sum it took to have their embarrassing affliction eradicated and he was certainly a millionaire many times over, living a life of extravagance and luxury.

Dr. Willie answered the phone and I got right to the point, explaining Priscilla's Manson-Face disease in graphic terms and pointing out how nice and pretty she was and how badly I felt about her problem. Dr. Willie perked up; he had heard of Manson-Face and was always eager to tackle something new and controversial. He told me that there were only 37 confirmed cases of Manson-Face and the nearest one besides Priscilla was in Longview, 130 miles away. The fact that Priscilla was basically forced out of her job because of Manson-Face only increased his excitement level.

I first met Dr. Willie in 1980 at a defensive driving class. He was a tall black man – well over six feet – with a muscular build that made him look like a football player or some kind of wrestler. We spoke a bit but didn't really hit it off until a couple of years later when he started working at a Subway that I used to frequent on a nearly daily basis. His title was "Sandwich Artist" but he was always more interested in counseling people about their relationships and advising people on their problems and concerns. His sandwiches weren't actually very good – he usually shortchanged you on the meat – but he was the most popular employee there because of his helpful proclivities. Everyone that went to that Subway requested for Dr. Willie to prepare their food even though it was fairly common knowledge that his hands weren't usually clean and he always seemed to have a touch of the flu. During the preparation, Dr. Willie would carry on a dialogue with the customer that would send them on their way with a smile and a song spilling from their mouth.

He didn't last very long at Subway but we kept in touch through the years; I was in awe of his intellect, yet very comfortable in his presence. I was confident that he would make his mark on the world in a very big way – he possessed that special and unique kind of talent.

Once he made the decision to begin dispensing medical services, Dr. Willie never looked back at all. That is to say that he dove in head first, acquiring an office, a pretty receptionist, plenty of the tools of the trade and a strongly written malpractice insurance policy. He began seeing patients in 1984 and, at his peak, was treating well over a hundred patients per day. He did not advertise at all, but word of mouth had elevated his practice to an unprecedented level of activity, especially for a Doctor without the degree.

Soon, however, Dr. Willie became bored with the mundane, every day nature of the medical practitioner business. Sure, he enjoyed helping people but helping folks beat their sniffles began to lose most of its appeal for him. He wanted to tackle bigger and more challenging problems, to assist those desperately in need instead of simply comforting the mildly uncomfortable. Dr. Willie decided that he would limit his practice to working with patients who had been afflicted with rare, horrible, disfiguring illnesses and diseases, desperate people who had been shunned by the medical establishment and had no place else to turn. He correctly predicted that he would make much more money this way and derive infinitely more satisfaction from his work.

Dr. Willie requested to see Priscilla the next day and we made an appointment for 2pm at his office. We hung up and I called Priscilla to give her the good news; she was thrilled. She told me that she had experienced a Manson-Face episode just a couple of hours earlier while getting a haircut. The salon workers had gotten really frightened and called the police. When the police arrived, she was still undergoing Manson-Face and they became really frightened and used pepper spray to punish her. Priscilla was quite anxious to be cured once and for all. Incidents like this were taking the life right out of her.

I picked up Priscilla at her efficiency apartment the following afternoon at 1:30 and we headed over to Dr. Willie's. She was ready – not the least bit apprehensive – and told me that she had a great feeling about all of this. We got to the office twenty minutes early and Dr. Willie escorted us straight into his office, bypassing reception and four mangled people hanging out glumly in the waiting area.

"Do you guys want any coffee or anything?"

Priscilla and I both shook our heads "no". Dr. Willie looked her up and down, seemingly searching for a clue or even a hook. She smiled nervously and glanced over at his handmade certificates hanging on the far west wall of the office.

Dr. Willie put both of his huge hands on Priscilla's girlish shoulders. "What do you actually know about Manson-Face?"

"I know it sucks. I know it's embarrassing and humiliating and it cost me a job. I know I can't keep a boyfriend and I know it's ruining my life."

"Uh huh. Is there any warning when an event is coming? Do you feel it coming on?"

"No, not at all. One minute I'm enjoying my day and the next minute I'm being pepper sprayed or arrested or berated or fired. Once it's happening, I know it's going on – I just can't do anything about it. I'm paralyzed inside my own head."

Dr. Willie nodded in affirmation. "I would really like to see an outbreak. About how often does it occur?"

"Well, almost every day. I guess about five or six days a week – and at all different times of day...no rhyme or reason. Happened to me yesterday evening at the hair salon. Day before yesterday, it happened at a Thai restaurant with a group of my friends and their friends."

"There *must* be a triggering mechanism for this," said Dr. Willie. "We've got to figure out the common denominator. If we can find out what is triggering this thing, I know we can beat it! I *know* it!"

We all sat in silence for a couple of minutes, then Dr. Willie spoke up. "I need you to disrobe for me young lady."

Without any hesitation, Priscilla started removing her clothing, which caught me off guard.

"Um...I'm just going to wait outside..."

"No!" Priscilla proclaimed adamantly. "I want you to stay."

"OK." I sat down on the fake leather couch over by a case full of thick and musty medical books, trying not to look directly at Priscilla as she unashamedly removed her blouse, jeans, shoes and socks.

"Bra and panties, too," said Dr. Willie and Priscilla immediately stepped out of her panties and deftly unhooked her bra, allowing it to flutter to the ground in front of her. Damn, this girl was a workout warrior without an ounce of fat anywhere to be seen, with her muscular, pear-shaped butt, washboard abs, broad swimmer shoulders and perky little stand-up breasts. Dr. Willie was becoming visibly aroused in his pants; the only reason I wasn't is that I had seen her Manson-Face and that kind of ruined it for me. But she did look seriously good out of those clothes – no doubt.

Dr. Willie stood looking into her eyes, whistling nonchalantly as if to regain his composure a little bit. If Priscilla noticed his arousal, she did not let on.

"Let me test a few of your critical pressure points," Dr. Willie said and placed both hands on her neck, one up under the chin and the other on the back below the scalp. He towered over the much smaller Priscilla and his huge hands completely engulfed her feminine neck. He moved his hands down to both of her shoulder blades and began what appeared to be a little massage, complete with wiggling fingers and sweating palms.

"Hmmm…OK. Let's see," Dr. Willie muttered to himself as he examined Priscilla. He brought both strong hands down to her breasts, starting on the outside and then fiddling with the remainder, including the obviously sensitive nipples. Priscilla emitted a nearly inaudible gasp or maybe a sigh as he spent several minutes examining this particular part of her body. She squirmed just a bit but continued to allow the doctor unabated access. He grazed his hands across her belly and knelt in front of her to focus on her vaginal region, with each of his hands reaching around back and clenching an ass cheek. He was down there for a good while and just as I was beginning to fear that I was witnessing a sexual assault, Dr. Willie jumped to his feet.

"I've got it! I know what triggers the attacks! I know, goddamn it!"

"You do? What is it?" Priscilla was nearly squealing with excitement.

"Yeah Dr. Willie," I chimed in. "What is it?"

"Priscilla, you consume way too much high fructose corn syrup. I can smell it coming from your pores. And your bowel movements are unregulated – what, two or three a week?"

"Yes," Priscilla answered meekly.

"You have a pea-sized virus clinging to a wall in your small intestines. This virus is responsible for any number of things – inaccurate bowling, bad driving, panoramic reactions and, if my theory is correct, Manson-Face."

"Wow!" Priscilla and I shouted in unison.

Dr. Willie continued. "I believe that if I can stimulate this virus in some way, I can trigger a Manson-Face outbreak. If I can do this, then it will prove that all we need to do is remove the virus to get rid of this hideous disease."

"How do you do that?" I asked.

"Manually," replied Dr. Willie and he started busying himself getting ready. He stuck a light thing on his forehead, kind of like you would see on a coal miner. He pulled a long, silver cylinder-shaped apparatus from his drawer and plopped it onto the desk. It was smooth except for what looked like hand-carved notches in the right side. It was also really long, maybe nine or ten inches – maybe a foot. Then he pulled several matches from a box and poured himself a cup of black coffee.

"This is the part of the job I hate," Dr. Willie said as he guided the naked Priscilla over to his desk and used his hands to bend her over forward, her face and chest lying flat and her butt sticking out in all its glory. He got on his knees behind her and used his bare hands – no rubber gloves for this doctor – to spread her butt cheeks wide open, exposing the tiny aperture. He began digging into it with his fingers, doggedly attempting to gain access and it wasn't easy. The harder he dug, the more Priscilla unintentionally resisted and it took a good five or six minutes of battle before she relented. Once he had things going his way, he grabbed the silver cylinder and began shoving it violently into her. She yelped like a battered prisoner and so did I; this was painful for her and it was hard for me to watch.

"Been a while since your last bowel movement, hasn't it?" Priscilla did not respond and Dr. Willie continued. "You're real clean. Makes my job a little less unpleasant." He kept pushing the silver cylinder into Priscilla until it had almost disappeared. She was a trooper, lying across the doctor's desk whimpering a little but not protesting at all. Dr. Willie was using the light thing on his head to help him peer in behind and around the silver cylinder and he kept pushing it until it simply wouldn't go any further. He worked down there for quite a while – fifteen minutes or more – and finally seemed satisfied that he had accomplished something or another. Dr. Willie got up from his knees and nestled his crotch up against Priscilla's backside which, though he was clothed, I thought was borderline inappropriate.

"If my calculations are correct, we should be witnessing a Manson-Face outbreak if the next few minutes."

It actually occurred in the next few seconds. Priscilla began trembling and Dr. Willie hastily pulled back off of her butt and stood aghast as her skin began crawling and cloudy fluid began dripping from her eyes. Priscilla let out what sounded like the roar of a lion and when she turned around, she was experiencing full-blown Manson-Face. Her face was extremely frozen and she looked *just like Charles Manson!* She appeared positively Satanic with running nose and drooling mouth and it appeared she might embark on a killing spree or manic exercise at any moment.

"Oh my God!" Dr. Willie was positively freaked out and his boner was long gone. "That's hideous! I've never seen anything like it!"

"Yeah," I chimed in. "I've seen it maybe a dozen times but you never really get used to it."

"It's just freaking unreal!" he continued. "How long does this usually last?"

"Probably around thirty minutes," I told him. "It's a pretty intense thirty minutes. She's had them last as long as four hours, I think."

"No shit!" He was staring at Priscilla, who was staring back at him – basically catatonic – and her skin appeared to be turning scaly with petrified granules. She began to reek of bleu cheese and white wine mixed with bodily function and not in a good way.

"But you think you can cure her, right? You've got this figured out."

"Oh, hell yeah. I know it's all about that intestinal virus. All I have to do is scrape out that virus – just scrape it right the hell out of there – and her Manson-Face should be cured."

"Dr. Willie, you're a goddamn genius…you really are."

"Just have her back here tomorrow afternoon – same time – and I'll scrape out that virus and cure your friend. No more Manson-Face. Do you think she would mind if I call in a reporter friend of mine?"

"If you cure her, I don't think she will mind anything you do."

I took off early from work the next day to take Priscilla back to Dr. Willie's office. She was thrilled – really stoked – at the thought of being rid of her horrible affliction.

"I've had Manson-Face since I was twelve. You just cannot imagine what it's like to deal with this, to wait for the next outbreak, to try to figure out the timing so that you'll know when you need to be at home alone. This disease has been the absolute worst thing in my life. I *hate* being linked with someone as evil as Manson and I really hate looking like him. Being rid of this thing will make me the happiest girl on the face of this earth or any earth."

We arrived at Dr. Willie's and he escorted Priscilla back to his examination room. A camera crew from a local television station was already back there waiting for them and I sat down in the lobby to chew on some fat with a couple of geezers. I didn't know how long the procedure would take and I was pleasantly surprised when the camera crew began filing out after just under an hour, telling us all that it was pretty gross but was all over now.

A few minutes later, a gingerly moving, slightly hunched-over Priscilla inched out of the examining room followed by a smiling, jovial Dr. Willie.

"We did it!" he announced to the receptionist, three old guys and me. "We made history in there! Medical science and the world as we know it will never be the same. Never!"

Priscilla put Dr. Willie's $3500 bill on her Visa and was indeed cured, never again suffering from Manson-Face, Nixon-Face or any other kind of face. She didn't come back to work at my company; instead she decided to go back to school to study gardening and architecture. We lost touch and I didn't see or hear anything of her for a long time, a period of several years. I also lost touch with Dr. Willie; he had become a big local celebrity after discovering a cure for Manson-Face and did the high society party circuit for a while before ending up in prison due to incurable IRS problems.

It did not come as a huge surprise to me when I got a wedding invitation announcing impending nuptials for Dr. Willie and Priscilla. In hindsight, I could see the chemistry between them, the animal magnetism that was evident in his office during her treatment. Priscilla had visited Dr. Willie in prison a few times and when he was released early for good behavior, the two of them hooked up. I did not go to the wedding but read about it in some of the local newspapers. It was a grand affair, lavish and regal, and was star-studded as well with plenty of the local rich and famous in attendance, from actors to athletes to news anchors to celebrity chefs. Judging from the pictures in the paper, Priscilla made a beautiful bride and Dr. Willie had evidently ballooned well past the 300-pound mark.

The last time I ever saw Priscilla was one night a couple of years after their wedding. I was in a drug store getting some prescriptions filled when I saw her coming down the aisle pushing a shopping cart loaded with candy and sponges. She was dressed in shorts and a tank top and looking great except for the fact that she now, for some reason, sported a wooden leg. One leg was real and one leg was wooden! I turned quickly away and, without delay, ducked out of the store and into the night. It was NOT reasonable to expect me to deal with all of that!

#12

Dirty Politics and the Law of the Lane

I WON'T LIE ABOUT it – I'm not very political at all and never have been. In fact, you could call me "politically asexual". I don't support Republicans and I don't support Democrats. I've only voted twice in my life and each time I voted for the candidates in the races who had the most exotic or fake sounding names. I don't see politicians as particularly talented or special or anything; in fact, I believe many of them to be criminals and many others to be beneath contempt and worse. If you cut open most politicians, you would find a rotten core and gooey fluids that could suck the very life out of you.

Call me naïve, but when I was presented with the opportunity to assist in developing ads for a political contest, I saw a chance to make the proverbial difference. This was a few years back and one of our local incumbent congressmen was in an extremely close battle to retain his seat. His senior staff hired me from a recommendation and I felt sure that it was because of my reputation as an earnest, creative and loyal wordsmith. I was so inspired that I went home the very night I was hired and composed a compelling and thoughtful commercial script championing the virtues and praising the record of our beloved candidate. I waxed poetic about his dedication to the community and his love of family and affection for God and the God-like images erected in his backyard. I felt that I had built a rock-solid case for the congressman and saw no way that any American could view my ad and not vote for our man.

My rude awakening occurred the next morning when I presented my work to the grizzled campaign manager. He freaking flipped and not in a good way. He screamed his hatred in blood-curdling volumes and called me a goddamned ignorant hack and a shit head Shakespearian moron. He hurled a paperweight, knocked an intercom off the hook and almost tore a phone book in two with just his nose. My guess at the time was that he was indicating that my script was "sophomoric". It turned out that the campaign manager was distressed because my ad was all about our candidate, with nothing at all about our opponent. I attempted to explain to him that I knew nothing about our opponent; I only knew what a great man our candidate happened to be. "Fuck that shit" is basically what he said – I needed to snoop and dig and invade and do whatever was necessary to find all the dirt I could on Mr. Opponent and then write a piece to smear him with it, especially around the eyes and lips.

I'm not sure if my disappointment was obvious to Harold the campaign manager, but I resolved to attempt to do things his way. Perhaps I was a bit green about political matters – after all, he'd been through the wars for over twenty years and I was still pretty snot-nosed. If Harold said I needed to find dirt on this guy, then I was satisfied that that was exactly the course of action I needed to pursue. Harold and a couple of the other campaign workers supplied me with the opponent's home address, office address, phone number, kids schools, favorite restaurants, favorite sports teams, favorites color and the name of his therapist's husband's bookie. They instructed me that nothing was off limits…that I needed to find information that would make a mockery of the opponent, his family, his neighbors and even his second grade girlfriend. "Devastating humiliation" was the unspoken goal and nothing less would do. I didn't feel great about it but I had been hired to do a job and I knew I had to see it through.

Not really knowing where to start, I just began hanging out around the opponent's suburban home for a number of days, watching his family come and go and pretty much learning their daily routines. The wife did not work but always left the house around 10:00am to run errands, which consisted of getting her nails done, a massage, grocery shopping, coffee and sometimes a stop at a sports memorabilia shop. The teenaged daughter went to a private high school and seemed to be hanging around with the wrong crowd, as I saw her and four or five of her friends doing drugs, stealing hubcaps and torturing small, squirming animals while skipping school. The eight year-old son also attended private school but seemed to be a decent kid who had nice friends and a really good and conservative haircut. The opponent himself kept to a very strict regimen of spending his mornings at the office and spending his afternoons glad-handing in public and then retreating to a supporter's anchored yacht with a bucket of chicken, a quart of beer and an armload of print media. On the surface, there did not appear to be a whole lot of ammunition here…at least not the kind of ammunition that Harold was demanding.

It was imperative that I dig deeper. I took to snooping through the family's garbage late at night, usually after midnight. I would steal the garbage and then take it back to my apartment for further examination. This yielded more than a few interesting tidbits. I found out that the couple's son had been adopted five years earlier from a single Arab mother who was a convicted felon in her native land. I discovered that the opponent was paying a sum of $500 per month to a land developer who was blackmailing him over some alleged human trafficking offenses. There were tons of liquor store receipts, doctor's prescriptions, department store surveillance tapes and photocopies of letters from a Chilean embassy. I also found autographed photos of Meredith Baxter-Birney and Corbin Bernson, shattered and bloodied eyeglasses, partially eaten flesh sandwiches and half a dozen sleepless nights.

As I began to peek into their windows at night, I found yet more dirt to work with. The candidate himself favored sitting down while peeing, which was a revelation and an indictment. His wife was constantly adjusting her plastic surgery with her hands and with utensils and whatnot. The teenaged daughter enjoyed providing blowjobs in her bedroom to vagrants and other endowed rascals, while she wore rubber gloves and hummed "Silent Night". The little boy was pretty much just doing his homework and stuff and not paying too much attention to the others in the house.

When I reported my findings back to Harold, he was clearly thrilled.

"You learn quick, don't cha? You've done real good here…real good! This is exactly the kind of stuff I was talkin' about." Harold was looking through some of the selected garbage and reading my first-hand account of what I had observed during my stakeout. "This guy is toast!"

"So Harold, do you want me to write up a script?"

"No, no...don't you worry about that. I've got someone for that. I just want you to keep doing what you're doing. You're my guy!"

This was puzzling. I thought they had recruited me to their campaign for my proven writing skills but instead they seemed to prefer me to work as a pseudo private detective, which I had never done before in my life. It had been sort of fun in the beginning with the coffee and donuts and binoculars and such but it grew boring in a goddamn hurry. I didn't really want to do it anymore but Harold could be intimidating and I decided not to make any waves. If the campaign wanted me to keep spying on this guy and his family, then I would keep spying on this guy and his family.

The next night was a Sunday, which I decided to skip. I drove back over to their house the following evening just after dark and took up a position across the street and one house down. The opponent's house was darkened for the most part and things seemed pretty quiet. The wife's car was in the driveway but his vehicle was not there. Wearing my dark clothing, I decided to slink my way to the bushes in front of their living room window. It was a decidedly tranquil neighborhood and I encountered no issues making my way up to the house. I mingled with the shrubs and tried to look into the window; the shades were drawn but there was a tiny crack of an opening where the two sides of the drapes were supposed to meet. Peering through this crack, I watched as the boy played video games and the mother was involved in a game of Twister with a man I had not seen before. I worked my way over to the daughter's window and her shades were left about eight inches open. She was inside on her bed with three burly black men who looked to be in their thirties or forties. The men were naked and I could barely see the girl, as the men had her pretty well surrounded, with just her feet and parts of her legs sticking out of the crowd. The men's blackened hips were gyrating in unison and I had seen quite enough of that.

"Enough of that!" I murmured to myself and broke back across the front yard and sprinted to my car. I wrote copious notes in the dark concerning what I had just witnessed and sort of hung out a while. The opponent drove up in his cherry red Continental about ten that night and walked into the house carrying a briefcase and what looked like a frozen turkey under his left arm. He was clad in a suit that cost more than my car and was wearing a top hat, which was a new look for him. I waited a few minutes and then made my way back up to their living room window. Peeking in, I saw the opponent, now wearing just dress shirt, slacks and socks, lying flat on his back on the carpeted floor while his wife and her twister partner from earlier in the evening sprayed whipped cream into his mouth and acted as if they were fixing to use him as a toilet. I wasn't going to wait around to see that.

"I'm not going to wait around to see that!" I said aloud and hurried back across to my car. This assignment was really beginning to take its toll on me. I considered myself a normal guy from a normal family who grew up in a fairly normal neighborhood. Here, I was witnessing a lifestyle that I could not imagine to be sane, that I could not imagine as real. I was genuinely sickened by the way this family lived their lives and it made me wonder about the plight of humanity, albeit in the most general of ways. I vomited twice out my car window, started my car and drove the hell home.

I got back to my apartment that night and clicked on the television, just looking for a little soothing local news and nothing more. What I saw was an evidently rush-produced campaign ad for our candidate. It superimposed the opponent's face onto a man that was supposedly peeing while sitting down. A distinguished narrator asked the question, "If this man pees while sitting down, what else does he do while sitting down? Vote for a man that will stand up for you in Washington, around the world and throughout the universe, including the bathroom!" My opinion was that our ad was in bad taste and I wasn't at all sure that we were fighting fair. But I had to believe that Harold knew what he was doing and that our candidate was the absolute right man for the job. It was incumbent upon us to make sure he got the job and to not worry about any toll or consequences. That was for later...much later.

When I switched on my television the next morning, I found that our opponent had evidently rush-produced his own ad. In his ad, he had superimposed our man's face onto an image of Hitler speaking to his rabid followers and pounding his fist for emphasis under a flapping Nazi flag. The gist of the ad was that our candidate secretly admired Hitler and did not mind the killing of innocent people if the cause was just. It was an outrage and I was really pissed. Our opponent was obviously upping the ante with his horrible attack and I became really curious as to how Harold would respond to this abomination.

At the bustling campaign headquarters that afternoon, I sat down with Harold and gave him everything that I had gathered from the previous evening. I told him about the weird game of Twister, the daughter's gangbang, the frozen turkey, the dark toilet playtime. Harold's eyes got big as saucers and he cackled like a wounded jaybird. Then he handed me an envelope; I opened it and there was a check for $250. He told me to keep up the productive work and that there was much more where that came from. And then he told me to get the fuck back to work.

I left the office but did not go to work that day. I wanted to wait until the next morning and then follow the wife around for her daily run of errands and bits. I arrived at the house the next morning at 8:10am and both of the family cars were in the driveway. About 45 minutes later, the wife came out the front door, a purse and two large brown paper sacks in hand, hopped into her car, backed out the driveway and headed off down the street. I eased my car in behind her and tailed her to the local florist, where she sat out front in her car for fifteen minutes but never went in. She left there and drove to a local park, got out of her car, skipped over to the swing set, sat down in a swing and began doing some swinging. And swinging. The opponent's wife was swinging dangerously high and I began to become seriously concerned for her, contemplating whom I would call if she became injured or got into any kind of trouble. After staying in the park until nearly noon, she left and drove to the sports memorabilia shop where she jumped out with her two sacks and rushed into the store.

At this point, I made the bold decision to go into the shop and attempt to interact with the opponent's wife. It was risky, yes, but I reckoned that I might extract some valuable information and there was no concern that she would have any idea who I was. So I got out of my car and entered the store, a door chime heralding my arrival as I walked through the door. The shop was pretty dark and was filled with sports photographs, trading cards, posters, autographed balls, pucks and bats. The opponent's wife was standing next to a man I assumed was the store owner in front of a glass counter and the two of them were examining the contents of her two bags, which appeared to be a collection of deceased fruit flies or maybe rubber ones – couldn't tell for sure. His hand was on her waist as they conversed and periodically dropped down to cup her denim-clad butt. It was obvious that some funny business was going on here and I decided that I just wanted out.

I walked up behind her and put my hands on both of her shoulders, startling her. As she whirled around to face me, I said "I just wanted to tell you that I loved you in "Logan's Run". I'll give you a holler on the 14ᵗʰ and buy you that cup of coffee I owe you." I turned around and headed out of the store, the chime announcing my desperately hurried departure.

Abandoning my quest for the day, I went home and jotted copious notes of what I had witnessed. While working on this, I saw a new ad for our candidate on television and, considering everything I had reported to Harold, I was perplexed, to say the least. The ad depicted our opponent as a friend to deceased turkeys everywhere. It indicated that he wanted his turkeys dead and that he ate turkey without any type of cooking or preparation. Dead, raw turkey was his first love, far ahead of his love for country or community. At the end of this black and white commercial, a man resembling our opponent was depicted playing a miniature golf match with a frozen turkey, complete with golf clubs and funny pants for both him and the turkey.

I immediately called the office and spoke to Harold, indicating to him that I doubted the effectiveness of the latest ad and wondering why he didn't use any of the more explosive material I had supplied him. He was actually pretty nice to me for a while, explaining that he wanted to keep some of the stronger stuff in reserve to be used closer to the day of the election. I told him I could buy that but the turkey theme seemed like a complete waste of time and money. Losing patience and such, he told me to fuck off and get back to work.

I continued to stake out the family home for the next couple of weeks and followed various family members around from time to time. The ads from both candidates grew increasingly more disturbing and distasteful and I began to feel terrible about my involvement in the campaign. Our ads painted the opponent as a racist, a hate-monger, a prostitute, a fancy boy, a feces consumer and a locksmith. His daughter's promiscuity and his wife's erratic behavior and latent homosexuality were exposed for all voters to see. His campaign directed attacks at our candidate, labeling him illiterate and pimply and calling him an animal trainer, an inept mechanic, a Mussolini disciple and a disco dancer. They threw rocks at our candidate's family as well, depicting his wife as a shoplifter and his 14 year-old son as a frustrated sexual predator with often frozen extremities.

My extreme disenchantment became clear to Harold and he relieved me of my duties, handing me $1000, patting me on the head and sending me on my fucking way. The election was only three days away and I'm sure he felt that they had plenty of material in the can and was likely fearful of me going soft on them. I had grown to hate the political process but had no regrets about experiencing what I had experienced...I really didn't.

I watched the election night returns on the local Fox affiliate and the race wasn't close at all – our candidate garnered 57% of the vote versus 40% for the opponent and 3% for some well-spoken but forgettable Libertarian candidate. In his concession speech, the opponent stated that he despised our candidate and would "see him in hell". In the victory speech, our candidate said that the opponent really did not deserve to live a full life and that his family possessed the morals of street level urchins. He also verbalized his mission to adopt the opponent's children to save them from the harmful debauchery they endured on a daily basis. During the televised speech, I could see Harold behind the newly reelected candidate, waving his arms triumphantly and drunkenly cussing a few of the interns – but in the nicest possible way.

I'm relatively certain that my experience with this campaign contributed to the sense of detachment I've subsequently felt towards politics and government. I'm not a rebel or anarchist or anything; I just find myself not caring at all. The candidate I worked for served his term but was ousted in the next election by an outspoken billionaire who knew how to spend his money with sheer effectiveness. After losing, he disappeared from the public eye and was only mentioned sporadically in the local gossip columns. The opponent we defeated endured a high-profile divorce and a wee bit of chemical endangerment. His children were not ultimately adopted by our candidate, but each suffered their own individual slings and arrows. The girl was impregnated a number of times by several strange men and even a couple of formerly famous ones. The boy started his own rock band, which led him down the pathway to devil worship and he soon became essentially tone-deaf and worthless.

It was December 3, 2003 when Harold was killed in a freak cell phone accident. It made all the local newscasts and even a few of the national cable news outlets. He had no surviving relatives to speak of and it was seen as humorous to many when his will revealed that he had left his entire estate to be split between Winston Churchill and Lady Asher. The four million in cash and property was eventually funneled to a fund that supported the introduction of high school kids into the political process through careful applications of drug-soaked feathers. Harold's picture adorned a wall at the entrance of North Mesquite

High School for many years and became a haven for graffiti, paw prints, natural gas and auto insurance quotes. That would have been a bitter pill for him to swallow but he would have swallowed it courageously and without hesitation.

#13

Y2K and the End of the Blow

I KNEW THIS GUY back in the day that was scared shitless about the arrival of the year 2000 or Y2K, as it was called. This man was normal in every other way imaginable: Good job, picturesque family, nice home with a well-manicured lawn, healthy love for church, pets and sports. Todd's parents had raised him right, teaching him the value of a dollar and the importance of striving to do the right thing whenever the right thing was appropriate. His wife Molly should have been in commercials; she was that earnest, that appealing, *that normal*. His two middle school-aged boys were both "A" students, star soccer players and seemingly friends to all. I had been at their house on numerous occasions and the boys had all types of friends over – jocks, babes, eggheads, nerds…even stoners. The entire family was welcoming and non-judgmental, making them extremely popular in their tight-knit community. Todd had even once briefly considered a run for the mayor's office – and he would have won, too – but he determined that fatherhood would be unjustly impacted by the stress and time requirements of the job.

As the late nineties wore on, I sensed that Todd had become detached, distracted. He was not his usual jovial self and my first instinct was that there must be some marital problems. This was hard for me to fathom because Molly seemed like the perfect wife, but I did not know how else to explain Todd's gradual and unexplained transformation into an unobtrusive, morose loner. We weren't "best friends" but we were close and I decided that he might need a confidant. I asked him to lunch at Hooters, hoping that he might open up a little about whatever it was that was going on in his life. He accepted but did so in such a damned muted manner that I thought he was on downers.

We met at the Irving Hooters on a Wednesday at around lunchtime. I preferred the Irving Hooters because the waitresses were ultra amazing and I always thought they must have a better oven there because the wings always came out with just the perfect amount of black and, as everyone knows, "black" is the key to a truly great wing.

"So Todd, I can tell something's up with you. You seem stiff...you don't seem yourself. You seem to be in some kind of unseen, unexplained pain. What's going on? What's happening with you?"

I could see him visibly tense up as I spoke. He was a prematurely gray man with soft, round features and his eyes seemed to almost pull themselves apart right in front of me.

"There's nothing wrong. I really don't know what you're talking about."

"Todd, it obvious there's something. I'm pretty goddamn perceptive in more ways than one. You know this about me. You're not the same guy. There's something..." He cut me off.

"I caught Molly having an affair with the lawn company."

"Huh? What? *What?*"

"I caught Molly having an affair with the lawn company."

"With the whole company?'

"I don't know. There were three or four of them in there. I couldn't stay in there to take a head count or anything."

We sat in silence for a while, staring into our cloudy, suddenly lukewarm beers. This was surreal! I could not believe that Molly would betray Todd like that. She seemed like the perfect wife; they seemed like the perfect couple! The more I considered it, the more this scenario seemed a complete impossibility. Yes, the more I considered it, the more I knew this was not true.

"Bullshit."

"What?"

"Bullshit, Todd. That didn't happen. Molly didn't cheat on you. I don't believe it for a second. No, there's definitely something wrong but that's not it. I've known you guys too long."

Todd looked up from his beer and grimaced. "Yeah, it's bullshit. I don't know...there's nothing wrong. Really, it's nothing."

"Bullshit. There's something wrong. Listen, if you don't want to tell me, that's fine. But I hope you get it worked out because it's wearing on you…it really is."

"OK," Todd said. "I'll tell you." He lowered his voice to barely above a sheepish whisper. "I've been doing a lot of research on this Y2K. I've also done my own calculations and compiled a few charts and graphs. I believe it's inevitable that the world as we know it is going to basically end. Poof! Vanish! And I want to do whatever it takes to protect my family. And that's going to mean roughing it, and I mean *really* roughing it. Anyone who stays in the cities will die so I'm planning to get my family out into the middle of nowhere and hopefully we'll avoid the tragedy. And mark my words…it *will* be a tragedy. Millions will die. Millions more will suffer and wish they were dead. You're going to die and your loved ones will die. This is going to be like the end of the dinosaur era. I'm telling you, I know it! I can feel it!"

"Yeah, the Y2K thing…I've heard a little about it, not that much. I mean, I heard it's gonna mess up some computers and stuff but how is…"

"It's ALL about the computers. Computers run everything. When the computers fall, mankind will follow. It MUST! Our society has married itself to technology and without the technology, our society will cease to function. There is no failsafe. I promise you that this will be a tragedy of biblical proportions – biblical!"

"So what are your plans for this?" I was curious but I was also getting a little bit bored and had been checking out some of the giggling Hooters girls who were dancing around the periphery.

"I started at the beginning of the year. I've been stockpiling water, canned foods, building materials and batteries. I've got a truck full of this stuff out back behind the house. We're going to find some space up in the Rocky Mountains, build a little house and just wait it out."

"You're gonna build a house? For real?"

"I've pulled some manuals off the internet. With the boys helping, it won't be too hard." He paused a few seconds. "You know, you're welcome to come. The kids and Molly wouldn't mind and we…"

"Oh no…no, no. Hey, thanks for the invite but I can't just uproot and do that. I mean, I've heard that it's really not gonna be that bad and all."

"Well, that's what the government wants you to think. Believe me, they're all planning to do the same thing that I am. They're gonna save their asses and leave you fools out in the cold. Just wait."

"OK." The conversation had grown tiresome and I changed the subject to how much the Cowboys sucked. My friend Todd seemed to have lost his mind. Was there a little bit of concern in my mind that things might turn bad on January 1, 2000? Maybe just a touch – but I certainly didn't see this as the end of mankind or society as we knew it. I figured it was possible that there could be some glitches and inconveniences but I also knew that the brightest minds on earth had been working on this thing for months, if not years. I just assumed everything and everyone would be fine, except for the criminals, hookers, crazies and anyone that was lactating at exactly the stroke of midnight.

Todd and Molly checked their boys out of school on November 15th, loaded up most of their belongings and headed for Colorado. The fact that they didn't put their house up for sale smelled like a hedge to me but they nevertheless seemed committed to a life of contentment in the wilderness. I had visited them at their home the evening before they departed and they seemed positively giddy about the adventure awaiting them. All four of them beckoned me to drop everything and go along, which I had zero intention of doing. They were convinced they would never see me again – since I would be dead -- and we shared long, drawn-out hugs at the end of the evening. I even managed to cop an unintentional feel of Molly and, though inappropriate, it wasn't too bad at all.

It was a few days before I heard from them. I remembered that Todd had mentioned that they would be trying to limit cell phone usage to attempt to conserve them, so I didn't worry too much. When Todd finally did call, he called collect from a payphone in Creede, Colorado. He reported that they had settled on a miniature parcel of land about twelve or so miles outside of Creede and they were currently living in a large tent while they constructed the house. Todd said that they were making good progress on the house and that the tent was comfortable because it was not very cold there, though he knew the weather would soon change. He also told me that one of the boys had driven a nail completely through his thumb and that Molly had been bitten on the ankle by some kind of fast snake.

I thought about the family a lot as the days counted inevitably down to the New Year. I called Todd and Molly's cell phones on a number of occasions during December but they never answered; it always went straight to voice mail and I don't know if they ever heard the intriguing messages I left for them. I decided to stay home on the big night and watch everything unfold on my television. Of course, by the time night fell, we already knew that Y2K was no big deal as New Years were celebrated uneventfully around the world in the hours before us. In Auckland, New Zealand they lined up inebriated waitresses to drink catsup from shot glasses at the stroke of their midnight, proving that even Y2K could not inhibit their genial silliness.

I was not sure if it was pride or prejudice, but Todd and his family did not return immediately. In fact, months went by with no sign of them. I attempted phone calls but I imagined that their phones must have died or something, as I got nowhere. I spoke with common friends; everyone was worried but generally felt that this level-headed family had likely landed on their collective feet. I decided to let it go and move forward with the eventful and scrumptious life I felt compelled to lead.

When the tragic news came, it was stunning. The family of four had been discovered dead by, ironically, a group of traveling gravediggers at their clay hut. The two boys were dead over a game of Monopoly. Molly was dead over a stove full of cheesy casserole and the like. Todd was dead over an eight-foot putt. The subsequent investigation uncovered that carbon monoxide poisoning due to inadequate ventilation had resulted in their evidently simultaneous demise and they hadn't felt a thing.

I spoke at their funeral service and lauded them for their sense of family and their genuine love for one another. I described their inner goodness and outer beauty in great detail, which set off a little bit of murmuring amongst the mourners. Then, for some reason, I wandered far off-script and blasted Todd for allowing his baseless fear of Y2K to put his family in that kind of serious jeopardy. I also criticized Molly for her lack of a daily workout routine and even let the boys have it for their substandard skin complexion. I don't know what got into me but I became a raving lunatic and went a little crazy before being pulled away by some weary pallbearers and their unattractive girlfriends.

The group hustled me out of the church and left me in the parking lot by a hearse, alone with my thoughts. I was already regretful about what I had said and was anxious to make amends but I did not know how to go about it. For lack of anything better to do, I pulled out my trusty pocketknife and slashed the hearse's two back tires. Then I looked to the sky, blew a kiss and got the hell outta there, scampering away like a badly wounded ostrich or something equally as erratic.

#14

• • • • • • • • • • • • • • • • • •

Moral Dilemmas and Thanksgiving Pie

I'LL NEVER FORGET A particular Thanksgiving morning – many Thanksgivings ago – when I woke up in a river…IN a river. It was wet and chilly and uncomfortable and to this day, I have no recollection of what happened or how in the hell I ended up there. I certainly didn't want to be in that river on Thanksgiving – would have definitely preferred to have been with family in a cozy home sitting over a robust meal. But I was unmistakably in a river and there was no changing that.

I do remember the night before participating in a focus group examining the effects of puppy breath on the human nervous system. There were 17 of us in the group and we met in a Spartanburg, South Carolina Winn Dixie meat cooler that doubled as a concert hall for the underprivileged. Our ten woman, seven man assemblage never got along from the beginning and we seemed destined to waste the disciplined efforts of six adorable puppies and of our celebrity group director, one half of Milli Vanilli. We squabbled about absolutely everything, from the clinking of glasses during a toast to a blemish conceal lotion developed especially for parrots (or orioles). One half of Milli Vanilli did his best to intervene when squabbles became shrill or physical but he simply could not keep up with the workload. One minute I was arguing with an intense twenty-something female tree climber about the relative merits of open-toed footwear and the next minute I was in a river.

I have no idea how long I was in that river. I guess I had been unconscious but was fortunate to have floated long enough to become snagged in some brush that jutted from the muddy bank. I was scratched and further injured by the jagged sticks and limbs but I was positively delighted that they had been there. I painstakingly extricated myself from the tangle and battled through the slowly flowing water in the direction of the shore. The bank slanted sharply upward from the river and it was so slippery that I had to crawl on hands and knees to get safely away from the water. I collapsed into a pile of leaves under what appeared to be a dead tree and lay there for a good while until I became aware of a nest of water moccasins some fifteen or twenty yards away. With the snakes so near, it was an uncomplicated decision to get passively to my feet and tiptoe off in the other direction.

I trudged through thick, whispering woods for an hour, maybe two, before happening upon a puny little country road with a black top and enormous holes. I had completely lost any sense of direction by this point and made an arbitrary decision to go to my left; it seemed suitable though I did not know why at the time. Later it all became clear; I was traveling in the direction of bright lights, warm food and a shadowy, back alley pharmacy.

#15

Poetry Found, Poetry Bludgeoned

I HAVE SEVERAL FRIENDS and acquaintances that are ALWAYS finding stuff. Noel possesses an uncanny knack to find money – and not just coins. He finds 1's, 5's, 10's…even the occasional 20 just lying around on the ground. Don't know how he does it but he simply does. Another friend of mine is Burton and he seems to always find drugs. Burton is not a drug-user or anything but damn if he doesn't always find prescription and illegal substances --and the *good* ones -- just here and there and around. Once Burton found an empty gallon milk container full of 2500 ecstasy tablets and he ended up selling them for whatever the going street price was – paid for his vacation to Europe that summer! Another time he discovered a bushel basket full of raw heroin, which he was able to parlay into part of a beach house in Pensacola or somewhere. My buddy Levi constantly finds love; he's became engaged to 13 different women and ended up marrying eight of them, including a distant relative of Gertrude Stein.

Me? I always seem to find poetry, often in the least likely and worst managed places. Sometimes the poetry is scrawled in a bathroom or dipped in chocolate. Other times the poetry is popping from a pan or bathing with a friend. But it's the thing I always happen to find and it ain't worth squat – it certainly ain't drugs or love!

Found this in the median of Texarkana's State Line Blvd while performing involuntary community service:

Tender mercy I send to my friend of all friends
Who suffers the pang of a devilish mark
With a dignity designed to placate the extinct.
Here aura is timeless but the burden is reserved
And the distress she sustains is an ill, scalding trial
That leaves her exposed in an ambiguous gleam.
The encouragement I proffer lands conspicuously shy;
My vocal assurances seem inadequate and trite.
She's an angel in a cross-stitched hat, a goddess in repose;
But resistant, she is, with an understated calm
To my impelling efforts to allay, to relieve.
I'd lay down my life with a deep, violent thrust
If it would remedy the distress, rectify the dissent.
And if the gates I encounter are pearly and bland,
I shall strike them with the force of an unsecured loan
And mourn the stumbling plight of my friend of all friends
While wearing a sheer costume not mean for a man.

Found this in the steam room at an Azle, TX blindfold manufacturer:

A pledged infestation, a plague in arrears
Guides chills up and down my form.
I struggle to fret amidst a temporal force
That had barged just ahead of the storm.
My love soars like Icarus far above the fray
Seeking mitigation of the stain.
The empathetic watch, the tentative grasp
Team to banish relegated disdain.
Free at last, my senses provoked,
My mouth frees up just the right space
To recite some words I've been longing to hear
And then flourish with little or no trace.

Found this floating on the surface of a water puddle inside a Hershey, PA
bait shop:

Studying the face, analyzing a subtle move or twitch,
I endeavor with vigor not to squander my mind to stone.

Woe descends into recesses like a bonnet-flavored foam,
Muting a dyslexic inner dialogue, applying preconceived malice
And bitter, eye-popping constriction (with a bit of a twist).
Probing with dignified fingers that aren't exactly mine,
I scour for redemption, of sorts, in an unintended privacy
Bereft of warmth or even a solitary, pliant splatter.
A feeble advance is met with a galaxy of sight and sound
That batters my stuff into embattled, disinclined submission
And greases a stunningly expeditious, unappreciated decline.
The sound of a voice trips me out like a banshee,
Melting me in ways a guy should never be melted,
Defining many convictions and tempting others still.
My mind is sprawled – defenseless – on a frosty base of smack,
Living for the moment, sure, but longing for deliverance.

Found this taped to a mallet in Poor David's Pub (I'm not usually allowed
in there but I wore a disguise):

A passionless pinch, a withering glare
And I retreat to my specialty box.
The clouds seem formed from a fruitless eve
And punctured with spirit-filled pocks.
Lofty walls recede in a frank withdrawal
While acknowledging the grief;
A hunter mulls an astonishing kill
That tests my resolve, my belief.
I twist the past in an impromptu gag
With the focus on a faith within;
The swiveling lie demonstrates itself
To be something more than a sin.
Heartbreak emerges from the soul of a saint,
Searching for the soul of another to taint.

Found this written on the restroom wall of the Casa Linda El Fenix
restaurant:

Using breathtakingly expansive, yet chillingly innate strokes,
You shaped and defined my deleterious, vulnerable being
With an essentially galling blend of cheer and amiable presence

That commandeered my thoughts…my sentiments (my dreams).
The void you left is awash with anguish but will be filled, no doubt,
By a swiveling, candy-laced something or another in bezel and bow
Which will believably uncover a fixation that does not digress,
A dark, searing thirst that can scarcely be quenched (in spades).
Living goes on in a series of petulant, mundane fits and starts
That serve to exacerbate distress within an inconsolable mind.
I'm left behind in a place where friendship possesses diminished bite --
A place of jacketed jesters, of portly gap-toothed mongrels.
Tears ooze gently, surely down prematurely tepid and spackled walls,
Pooling agreeably at the base of processed shame and dexterity,
Betrayed, I have been – by my own wretched and unimpeded ideals
Which devoutly convinced me that you (or someone like you) was real;
Really real.

Found this in a freezer at Dairy Queen next to the Dilly Bars:

Convicted of an atrocity I could not commit,
Sliced in two halves for challenging a substandard fate,
I trail a bright clan for a couple of hundred miles
To discover redemption and a hard-earned peek.
Romping, I get bashed to reality by a figurative palm
And tend to an urgency that just won't let me be –
That won't allow history to perish like an unfit willow.
Parched resilience sops up embers of a once-lavish style,
Negating an unconvincing prayer I offer with a two-faced mouth.
An untruth is told but "they" won't let me hear,
Preferring me be stranded in uncompromising darkness
With a mountain of unmitigated guilt peppered by mandate.
I scour for parcels of undercover affection,
The beauty turning down and my eyes growing faint.
(And I need that like I need a hole in the head).

There are a thousand more, maybe two thousand (maybe three thousand). I have found them in a window at the Freddie Mac headquarters. I have found them hidden in the compositions of Florent Schmitt. I have found them in all of the world's major cities with the exception of Warsaw and Tulsa. I found them submerged in vats of leaven and I have found them wedged in the fins of mudskippers. The last time I attempted to count them, I was at home alone on a Saturday night and lost a thrush in my ear, which caused me to abort prematurely. But at least I didn't cry…at least I didn't cry.

#16

● ●

Escape From Afghanistan... Unconventionally

THE SAD TALE OF another friend of mine called Austin reduces me to tears whenever I think about it too much. He was but an innocent victim in what amounted to nothing short of gross international warfare. He was betrayed by his friends, family and possibly his government in ways that would boggle even the most jaded and cynical minds.

Austin possessed the rare gift of being able to throw his voice. He could say something and make it sound like it was emitting from a spot up to thirty feet away from him – in real time. It was totally cool! I have no idea how he did it but he could do it at any time except when he had a head cold (or when he was wearing pretty stockings) and the results were usually hilarious. We would play practical jokes on unsuspecting strangers with Austin throwing his voice to a statue or little baby or an otter and the reactions of these people would just kill us! This gift also rescued him from some tough situations when he was about to be beaten or when he was being audited or reprimanded for general foolishness.

Austin was an extremely nice man, giving and charitable, and he didn't deserve the cruel fate that befell him. It turns out that suspected members of the United States government had placed him under constant surveillance and had been following him around for a period of several years. They had determined that his skill might be useful in some of their international conflicts and had been analyzing his behavioral patterns to gauge compatibility in relation to the required assignments. It had become a foregone conclusion that Austin would be abducted by his own "government"; all that was left to be decided was when and by what method.

What the "government" did was utilize three of their "agents" to infiltrate Austin's small, tight circle of family and friends. Once they had become trusted, the agents informed his family of their plan to abduct Austin in the interest of national and global security and even enlisted their help in the underhanded process. One weekend night, Austin's parents lured him to a local boat ramp with the promise of salted cashews where the waiting agents gassed him and went on to perform hypnotic alteration. He was transported to a top-secret installation in Jefferson City where he was held against his will and trained in the fine art of deception. The plan was to use Austin's ability to throw is voice to carefully place inflammatory and controversial statements into the mouths of the leaders of several unfriendly countries and radical groupings. If successful, this might poison the mood of the population in these enemy lands; if unsuccessful, Austin would most likely be tortured, dismembered and even killed.

He was put through intense physical training as well as diplomatic and world history studies. He was also forced through grueling sessions designed to enable him to master nearly seven foreign languages. Austin was beaten into submission on thirteen different occasions and his diet was altered to such a degree that he lost way more than twenty pounds. He was commanded to grow a goatee and shave off his eyebrows on a semi-daily basis. Using mind control techniques, these suspected members of the United States government turned my friend Austin into a captive robot slave, capable of almost nothing except blindly following their manipulative leadership – and, of course, pooping.

Austin's first assignment was not generally dangerous; his handlers evidently wanted to put him through a "test run". He was given credentials and sent to a speech by the English Prime Minister to a group of honored primary school children, the crux of the speech being the importance education plays in professional life and beyond. During one pause when the prime minister was taking a drink of water, Austin threw his voice to the prime minister's podium and spoke clearly into the microphone about education being "for the birds" and how David Beckham was such an "alluring man with real, working muscles." The prime minister was startled and looked about feverishly trying to figure out what was going on while the room chuckled nervously. Later, when a child was asking the prime minister for advice on dealing with bullies, Austin threw his voice into the microphone, abruptly cutting off the little boy with a terse "Man up, son. Sometimes you must let your fists do your talking, even if they are small." The boy burst into tears while handlers rushed the prime minister from the room, never figuring out that Austin was the culprit.

His next assignment came in Berlin where the German chancellor was addressing a large crowd of citizens on the continuing worldwide threat of terrorism. Austin procured a spot near the front and waited for a certain delectable opportunity. When the chancellor turned his face away from the microphone to cough or to stifle a cough, Austin – in his newly learned German – threw his voice into the microphone. "Long live Bin Laden and snuggle Hitler, as far as I'm concerned...you freaks!" The chancellor was forced to retreat to a small room behind the stage as the crowd grew instantly rebellious and insulting and began hurling expletives as well as projectiles at the stage area. He was actually trapped back in that room for two hours until the military fired tear gas and brandished killer batons to quell the outbreak.

Less than a week later, Austin was dispatched to Milan, Italy to attend a speech by the city's chief of police regarding a recent upturn in violent crime in the city. The chief bemoaned the increased violence and threatened the responsible parties with prison terms, lashings and worse. During his third dramatic pause, Austin threw his voice to the chief and announced – in the chief's voice – "I am a cross-dresser, a serial rapist and a merry potted planter" (his Italian was still not quite right). The chief was stunned to immediate stillness and silence; then, confused, he ran from the podium as tears began falling and wails began hurtling from deep within his inside places. An angry mob of Italians formed in the street and began setting fire to cars, garbage cans and hair while clomping up and down sidewalks with their gaudy Italian shoes. The chief ended up losing an arm and the majority of his dignity in the continuing violence. And once again, Austin got away scot-free.

I guess the powers-that-be had determined that Austin was ready and sent him into a dangerous section of Afghanistan. He was disguised as a peasant while some Taliban lieutenant spoke to his troops, spinning a yarn about evil Americans, unfair capitalistic practices and the hidden dangers of diet soda. When the time was right, Austin threw his voice to the lieutenant in the native language and proclaimed all Americans "very pretty and savory and full of honey" and all Canadians "music-filled angels full of warmth and funny little ribbons". The men looked at the lieutenant sideways while he looked back at, them angry and puzzled.

"What was that? That wasn't me! That wasn't me!" The lieutenant realized right away that he was a victim of some kind of curious espionage. He furiously stared down the troops and spewed venom that could kill a hundred men. "I want to know who is responsible for this! I demand to know who is responsible for this act of treason! Speak to me now or die later."

Everyone began shifting uncomfortably and murmuring very quietly among themselves. Austin asked one of the soldiers why the lieutenant was so hostile about an obvious joke.

"His entire family was killed by Americans. Americans once captured him and performed unnecessary brain surgery and then mocked him for the resulting twitches. They taunted him over his lack of coordination and shining ears. He wants to kill Americans here, in their homeland and all around the world."

Being robotic, Austin was not able to quit while he was ahead and just had to throw another comment from the lieutenant: "Who said that? I said that! And I love hairy men in starched white shirts and tugboats and marsupials."

This time, Austin's luck ran out. The soldier with whom he had been conversing saw his mouth moving during the comment and started leaping around crazily, pointing at Austin. "It's him! It's him. This is the dirty dog that mocks our leader. This is the mocking criminal!"

Austin acted all shocked and whatnot but the jig was undoubtedly up. The lieutenant stomped down from his platform and marched righteously up to my friend and got in his face, poking his index finger hard into Austin's chest.

"So little man, you have the courage to mock me?" He was spitting as he spoke and it hit Austin in the eyes and some even landed unfortunately on his lips. "Then you have the courage to die! I will not be made a fool by the likes of you. This much is true and I say it with all my heart."

Austin attempted a bit of futile denial but his grasp of the language betrayed him a bit. "I am not the man to whom you speak. I have honor on the playing field and would never dishearten the mind of another. I love you thusly and would have your diseases if medically possible."

"Take him!" Guards with guns and chains descended upon Austin and took him to a homemade jail. The next morning, he was paraded before a Taliban assembly, many of whom hurled coins, crock pots and lozenges. He was sentenced to death but with a sporting twist: If he could survive five minutes of hanging, he would be cut down and allowed to return home.

The hanging took place at sunset in a clearing outside a small Afghan village. It was a brutal affair; Austin was given no last words, no blindfold and no opportunity to run the hell away. He was escorted up the stairs to the hanging platform by a couple of female villagers, his hands tied behind him with thick, itchy rope and the assembled mass of soldiers hooting and jeering. The two ladies were both heartily massaging his penis through his pants, attempting to arouse him for the benefit of the show and it worked just a little bit but not quite fully. On the platform, the noose was placed around his neck and tightened like the dickens. My friend started a prayer but before he could finish, the floor beneath him fell out and his mad struggle began. His legs whirled like Janis Joplin on a vibrating Schwinn and the pain in his neck and head was crushing, excruciating. For the first thirty seconds or so, he was thinking clearly and was consciously considering the potential of staying alive for five minutes, forcing his chin down hard against the rope on his neck in an attempt to relieve the pressure. Eventually, though, he just wanted it over – real bad.

A couple of minutes into it, a miracle or something happened. The pain went away completely and a feeling of outright euphoria engulfed Austin. He thought that maybe he was dying and that God was taking pity on his plight. Turns out, he wasn't dying and it seems his body had miraculously adjusted to the hanging and it was in extreme survival mode. The five-minute mark came and, true to their word, the Taliban soldiers cut him down. The mocked Taliban lieutenant was incensed but obviously impressed.

"Get your ass out of my land. If I see you again, you will be shot through the head many times. Your will to survive is impressive indeed but you will not survive another meeting with me. Go!"

And Austin went, wandering through the stark Afghan wilderness for days and eventually somehow crossing into Pakistan. He lived on creek water, insects and beets and was on the verge of giving up when he came across a village with an American doctor, who treated him and contacted an American diplomat. The diplomat arranged Austin's transport home, where he was greeted by a group of delirious friends and family. Unfortunately, the ordeal had left him with slight to moderate brain damage; his memory was bad, his speech was impeded and he had difficulty controlling the left side of his body. He had also lost partial control of bodily functions and had "accidents" more often than a newborn. The path of his life had certainly been altered by the horrible ordeal.

After some digging, I was able to discover that the people who abducted Austin were not part of the United States government at all; turns out, they were members of a militant Islamic gang of thugs who were bent on embarrassing our country in front of the world and reportedly the universe. I uncovered the fact that they worked out of a back office in a Dallas-area convenience store and passed this information along to an FBI agent I knew from dance class. He assured me he would check it out though I can't be sure if he ever did. I do know that the store closed down after getting caught in a sting for selling alcohol and cigarettes to minors and their little brothers. It was the centerpiece of a story done by a local television investigative reporter and I was happy to see them getting embarrassed -- served 'em right and all that.

My friend lives with his parents, who attend to his daily needs the best they can. Of course, they are elderly and it's inevitable that he will one day end up in some kind of assisted living center. When I visit, some days he knows me and other days he doesn't. As sad as that might be, that's just the way it is and it's all for the best, I suppose. On almost every visit, I ask him to throw his voice – just for old time's sake and grins – but all that ever comes out of his mouth is a meek "heehaw".

#17

Dreams, Gravy and Howard Hughes' Innards

SOME YEARS BACK IN the very year I turned forty, I suffered through a three-week spell of the worst, weirdest dreams imaginable – some were even ominous. I don't know if it was the stress of turning forty or some other mitigating factor, but the dreams coming out of my head were wild and disturbing, the type of dreams you *never* share with another sane or conscious person. I considered getting some dream analysis conducted but feared the short-term exposure and ultimately feared what those dreams might be saying about me in no uncertain terms.

I "celebrated" my fortieth birthday in a valley of cleavage and the next twelve days passed uneventfully. On day thirteen, I had the first of the freaky, freaky dreams. In the dream, I was not a man – I was a carrot and I was wearing a lime green Speedo with frill around the edges. I was swimming in a competitive race against a tomato and a potato. I was in lane three, between the tomato in lane two and the potato in lane four. We were swimming the 100-meter freestyle and the potato took the early lead with the tomato and me in hot pursuit. I made up ground on my flip turn at fifty meters and pulled even with the potato while the tomato fell slightly off the pace. We came to the last ten meters stroke-for-stroke, looking one another in the eye on each breath. At the end, I managed to utilize the length of my carrot body to barely out-touch the potato for a truly treasured victory. I completed the race in 53.27 seconds, versus 53.59 for the potato and 58.77 for the tomato. I climbed out of the pool and was hoisted upon the shoulders of a mess of artichoke and since I had no shoulders, the medal they put on me fell straight down off my body to the floor, unfortunately taking my Speedos with it.

The very next night, I dreamt that I was in a fistfight with 1950's Marlin Brando for the affections of 1980's Jessica Lange. He wasn't as tough as I expected him to be and for a while it was an extremely competitive fight. I knocked him down with a right hook to his face; he hopped up quickly and floored me with a kick to the groin. I struggled to my feet and lunged at him, grasping him in a bear hug and taking him down to the ground. Marlin and I rolled over and over maybe a dozen times before wedging against an anchored wall in a festive saloon. I grabbed his hand and bent his fingers backwards violently and he began begging for mercy in a queerly girlish pitch. I told Marlin that begging was not becoming and that 1980's Jessica was now mine, whether he liked it or not. Marlin retorted that I was a brute and that he didn't particularly care for brutes and the like. The dream ended with Marlin Brando sobbing inconsolably into a beige handkerchief and pleading pathetically for one of his mothers.

The following night was a Wednesday and I had consumed an inordinately spicy meal of Mexican and Indian cuisine soaked in cream gravy and topped with frayed celery sticks. My dream was set in a downtown sandwich shop where I sat at the counter beside the singer Meatloaf (this dream was obviously triggered by a real-life encounter I had with him in a downtown diner). He was a huge, beastly man who consumed his foot long sandwich in less than thirty seconds. He became irate due to his dissatisfaction with the food and threw a chair with one hand while picking his nose with the other. Meatloaf's face was contorted in anger as he spewed expletives and insults in the direction of the cook, the cashier and a group of cowering patrons, which included me. I soon had seen quite enough and stood to confront the seriously pissed-off singer. I got right in his bloated face, grabbing his collar with both hands, and told him that if he didn't settle down I would criticize the constitution – his constitution -- in more ways than one. Meatloaf began shaking with hatred and then, nearly unbelievably, transformed into a life-sized Liza Minneli, complete with lipstick and tear gas. She told me that she had misplaced her Jack Russell terrier and that I might be her soul mate. Liza removed her top and began systematically thrusting her sagging chest in my direction; I woke up just in the nick of time.

Thursday night, I stayed up late with a book I could not put down and ended up going to bed well after 2am. My dream found me in a lukewarm bubble bath with a glass of white wine and a bowl of melted vanilla ice cream. The wine turned to sweat and the bubbles turned to sea turtles, which began biting me around the face and hands with teeth that were all too real. I sprang to my feet to escape the bath but found my escape blocked by Bonnie Franklin and two muscle-bound security guards dressed in black. I attempted to push through but the three of them began sexually assaulting me in ways I am reluctant to describe. Once I got their mouths and privates removed from my skin, I brushed past them, covered myself with a gold-plated towel and thumbed my nose at a society I just could not comprehend anymore.

I went to bed early on that Friday night, still exhausted from staying up late the night before. I was hoping for a dreamless sleep but it was not to be. I found myself in the middle of the battle of the Alamo, hunkered down with 180 or so Texans under siege by the superior, well-trained Mexican army. Now, I had done a term paper on the battle of the Alamo and my contention has always been that the performance of the Texans, while courageous, was overrated. There is no doubt in my mind that the Mexican army could have won that battle on day one had they chosen to do so. The fact that the battle lasted thirteen days is not a testimony to the skill of the Texans but more an indictment on the indecisiveness and ineptitude of Mexican General Santa Ana.

Anyway, there I was with an unwieldy musket, right in the middle of everything. I'm not sure what day of the siege it was but it seemed to me that they had already been there a few days. I saw Travis. I saw Crockett. I saw Bowie and Dickinson. I saw the Taylor brothers. I saw Baker and Bonham and Mitchell and Daymon and Holloway. I recognized them all right away. But I was not prepared for the way these legendary men conducted themselves, the way they treated each other. There was not much going on with the battle and I guess the inevitable boredom had set in. Oh, there were a few volleys back and forth and potshots here and there but the Mexican army was not yet serious and that was obvious to all of us in the mission. We could see them out there in the distance, dancing and singing and prancing and carrying on, seemingly oblivious to the men in the Alamo.

So a number of the men in the Alamo sought to entertain themselves in ways that I found to be unexpected, to say the least. Many of the men began making love to each other, some behind closed doors and some right out in the open. I was walking across the courtyard and I had to step around these guys all over the ground just *drilling* each other. And Crockett was right in the middle of everything, doing lots of drilling and even getting drilled a little bit. He also organized "rape" squads to terrorize the men who attempted to avoid the male-to-male contact and I saw these squads absolutely tear up their outnumbered victims. Travis had a male lover; Bowie had two of them and they all got after it in Bowie's room until he could no longer participate due to illness. I mean, I know these men had been without women for a long time, but this was insane! I even had to pull Crockett off a guy just to get him to his post as the final attack was beginning to unfold. Unreal! Luckily for me, none of them seemed to notice me and I was never raped, sodomized or assaulted. And also, luckily for me, I woke up just as a tiny Mexican soldier was pointing his bayonet my way during desperate hand-to-hand combat. What a nightmare it was for me to see the iconic men of the Alamo cavorting around and conducting themselves in such a manner!

The next night, I went out with a couple of friends to the zoo and then on to a rave of sorts, comprised mainly of middle-aged folks and candy salesmen. One drink led to another and that one led to still another. It wasn't long before I was fast asleep in a damp and drafty gutter having an esoteric dream. I was on an unsteady bar stool getting a haircut from Morgan Fairchild and a pair of sympathetic park rangers. I only wanted a little bit off the top but Morgan chopped it way too short, revealing portions of the left side of my brain. She was apologetic but that didn't stop the pouring rain that was sloshing about between my brain and a hard place, smoking like a top-heavy sailor. I couldn't afford the required treatment to fix the problem and was forced to settle for a half-baked shortcut involving a razor blade, some pills and a gap-toothed intern. When I awoke the following morning, lying in a gutter of my own filth and the filth of others, it occurred to me that I really *did* need a haircut but I resolved to see a professional stylist and not an unemployed celebrity.

Sunday night brought a dream that was oddly animated. I was eating at a long cafeteria table with twenty or so cartoon people, animals and things. I don't believe that I was animated but everything around me, from the spinning ceiling fans to the out-of-service vending machines, looked hand-drawn by an artist of at least limited ability. As I looked up and down the table, I saw Hulk Hogan, Betty Rubble, Salman Rushdie, Joey from Friends, Joan of Arc, a soiled stocking, Colonel Sanders, a giant octopus and Arnie Becker from LA Law. The colors of the drawings were vivid and life-like and started hurting my eyes, much like tiny little needles. Arnie Becker was having unconventional sex with Betty Rubble, while Salman Rushdie and Joey from Friends were discussing a possible business venture that would involve body piercing and Norm McDonald. Everyone at the table was eating toasted beef and their sister-in-laws but nobody seemed to be using napkins or anything remotely sanitary. In a fit of rage, Hulk jumped up from his chair and turned over the table, dumping everyone's food trays and sisters-in-laws onto the gravel-covered floor while chanting a wordy bohemian rant from a repudiated Broadway play.

All day Monday, I was in bed with a fever of 102 and a cough that chose not to quit. I had some chicken soup for lunch and a grilled cheese sandwich for dinner and didn't leave the house for any work or obligations. It was a relaxing day but that did not help in regards to my dream that night, which was another surreal one. I guess I was at home (or some place safe) and ordered a pizza. Ten minutes later, my pizza arrived, delivered by Nicole Kidman and Dabney Coleman. They were dressed in orange jump suits and wore hats made of banana peels and were very aggressive in pursuit of a tip. Nicole smelled like cough medicine and Dabney smelled like Yoda from Star Wars and they both tried using their fingers to win my affection (or at least my loyalty). I had no money but gave them throwing stars as compensation for the pizza and invited them to sit down for a slice. Dabney declined but Nicole wanted to hang out a little while longer. She ate four slices of pizza and began cleaning the carpet and the bathrooms. Then she did my laundry while showing me some blemishes on her chest and back. The blemishes weren't ideal but they weren't all that unappealing – maybe just a bit distracting. Dabney came back in and fetched Nicole, telling her that they had fifty more deliveries to complete. Nicole kissed my elbow with reverence and said that maybe we should meet again. I told her that I doubted it because of her persistent nervous tic, which I found distracting.

The next night, I was a fly on the wall during a momentous summit in a Las Vegas hotel room between Howard Hughes and Walter Matheau.

The two were discussing a movie project that Hughes wanted to produce about his own life and he wanted Matheau in the starring role. They had not previously known one another but really hit it off, with Hughes putting Matheau in a frisky, friendly headlock and mussing his hair and Matheau playfully clipping Hughes' overgrown, infected and unpainted toenails. The two shared a lunch of onion soup and Fritos and as they finished up, Hughes suddenly became irate and transformed into a moderate sized evergreen with precipitation dangling from its growth. A startled Matheau lunged for the door but did not quite get there before his skin melted away and his hair fell out in a heap.

The weird dreams kept coming in waves for the following couple of weeks. I had dreams about oil drilling amazons, football players without feet, hospitals for acme bricks, mansions without bathrooms, corn-flavored soda pop, a candy bar named "Mega Shit", mutilated ladybugs, handbags full of cocoa and a movie about migrating peacocks. I had a two-night full color epic about a Presidential election between Republican Leif Garrett and Democrat Detlef Schrempf. I had abbreviated dreams about kiwi-colored sunglasses and Afrin Nasal Spray. I even found my daydreams trending towards the bizarre with thoughts of car wash facilities constructed exclusively from Legos, hungry alley cats that traded on Wall Street and restaurants that served nothing but salt and ice cubes.

It seems that forty was affecting me much more adversely than I had ever imagined it would. I tried telling myself that it was just a number, it didn't mean anything, but the message was getting somehow lost in translation. I resisted the urge to seek professional help and instead confided in a steel worker I knew named Raul, who suggested that I use an adhesive to plug my ears before bed each night. When that failed to work, Raul recommended that I drape myself in an American flag and recite page 40 of five different Faulkner novels at bedtime. This actually did the trick temporarily and I experienced four consecutive nights with either dreamless sleep or dreams I could not remember. But when the fifth night produced a dream about a lactose-intolerant Sassanian, Raul decided it was time for something more drastic and told me about a book called "Theoretic Sleep and Other Theories" written by a relative of Marshall Faulk. He said this book addressed my specific problem, advising that people with vexing dream problems should avoid Steve Martin movies at all costs and needed to find common ground with people kept alive by machinery or other artificial means.

I followed the directions outlined in the book and soon found my dream problems to be solved. I was still having dreams but was not often remembering them. When I did remember them, they were normal, usually involving tall buildings and the Madonna. I soon adjusted to life in my forties and even came to relish the passing of years in much the same way that a heroin addict relishes a thick pack of the smack. And bedtime became the perfect conclusion to a day filled with smarmy mixed tapes and ill-fitting footwear.

#18

Sermon On the Mound

I BECAME ACQUAINTED WITH a pretty high-profile television evangelist through a mutual friend and the two of us hit it off really well. I had flown by his show a few times while channel surfing and I had speed-read his book about the non-negotiable requirements of the Lord, so I was impressed when he turned out to be a normal, everyday guy away from his profession. We hung out for cold beers, shot pool and even threw pointed darts at stationary targets on more than a number of occasions. I also met his wife and she was attractive and sweet and loyal -- just like she seemed on the television. The couple had no biological children but the evangelist was fond of saying that all of his followers were his children and he loved them like the dickens.

I could never forget the time he and I were sitting in an East Dallas bar in the early morning hours, drinking gin and tonic with extra lime and a dash of salsa when we were approached by a couple of pathetic, retched souls who recognized him from television or the news or somewhere. They hovered over us, alcohol poison literally streaming from their pores, and began taunting the evangelist in most unholy ways.

"Hey, look at this fucking Jesus freak," said one of them aloud, evidently attempting to alert the entire population of the bar.

"He loves Jesus and God," the other chimed in. "I bet he wants to be in bed with them."

"You know he does!" shouted the first.

The evangelist was totally nonplussed. He stood up from his wooden barstool and turned to face the two, towering over them. They were obviously taken aback because he didn't look all that big on television and they themselves had probably been physically shrinking from all the drugs and alcohol that they ingested.

"Friends, I *am* a Jesus freak. I *do* love God and Jesus. And yes, every time I have sweet sex, I'm having sweet sex with God and Jesus because they're inside *all* of us…you, me, my wife, Nolan Ryan, Tom Bosley… all of us. And I'm not ashamed of my love for God and Jesus. God and Jesus have been good to me. Why? Because I have allowed them to be good to me! I've welcomed them into my life and I interact with them *every single day.* I may not know what each day holds in store for me but I know they are with me and I know that I'll live with them in their big, magnificent mansion in heaven when I am dead and gone from this earth. Friends, join me. Take God's hand and let him deliver you from your despicable existence. Do it!"

The evangelist held both of his hands out, beckoning the two drunken men to grab hold. The men looked at the hands and then looked at each other, unsure of what the hell was going on. Finally, one of them very tentatively placed his hand in the evangelist's hand. The evangelist grabbed it up firmly and closed his eyes for full effect. Then the other man meekly took hold of the evangelist's free hand and the evangelist pulled both of the men in very close to him.

"Friends, we are not three men holding hands like queers in a bar. God and Jesus are in me. You are holding the hands of God and Jesus and you will revel in their strength. Friends, when you go to bed tonight I want you to pray. Pray hard. Pray like you've never prayed before. Ask God and Jesus to watch over you and help you escape your ridiculous and silly lives. Ask them to deliver you from your dangerous addictions and bless you with the array of goods that they keep readily available for souls such as yourselves. Can you do this for me?"

Both men nodded solemnly.

"Good! Now buy my friend and me a drink. Because when you are buying us drinks, you are buying God and Jesus drinks. They are within us!"

The men dutifully pulled out their wallets and paid for another round. The evangelist was smiling like the cat that ate the canary (or some other type of tasty bird).

"What's so funny?" I asked him.

"I just stole both of their watches," he whispered back, stifling a chuckle as he took a huge swig of his free drink.

We hung around a lot in those days and became really close friends with much in common: We both loved sports, rock music, Susanna Hoffs and The Ticket. We both despised computers, fire extinguishers, windy days, windy people and portable toilets. He and I would frequent a few of the local hangouts and would often go to see the local professional sports teams in action. He had a lot more free time than you would think and I was surprised at how little attention he appeared to pay to his ministry and the television show. The evangelist always seemed available to do something fun, no matter how late the notice or how insignificant the event. I really don't remember him ever saying "no" to anything, which seemed pretty unusual for a man of his status.

He was a fairly average looking middle-aged man, graying on his temples with a decent mid-life paunch, yet he was always drawing rapt attention from the opposite sex, mainly, I'm certain, because of his pseudo celebrity status. I sat and watched on numerous occasions as the women threw themselves at him in clubs, at games and even at stoplights. The more I observed the evangelist, the more I suspected that he possessed a deep and intense – and maybe dangerous -- dark side. There was just something about the glint in his eye as he dealt with people from all walks of life that gave me cause for concern. Was he a man of God? Certainly. Only a man of God could make people feel the way he made them feel about themselves and about each other. Was he a major league sinner? Signs were beginning to point toward "yes".

Not only had I discovered that the evangelist was prone to steal things, but I had caught him in the act of having public sex with a dozen strange women – in cars, in bathrooms, on pool tables. And he began to patronize streetwalkers on Harry Hines Blvd., paying twenty a shot for unprotected relations with these dangerous and filthy women. It was obvious to me that his demons were starting to get the better of him and his reckless behavior threatened to ruin everything he had built, everything he stood for. I sat down with him in the lobby of a vacant office building, determined to help if it was at all possible.

"You really need to cut out the crazy behavior – the stealing, the fornicating. If you're not careful, some investigative reporter is going to get a hold of this stuff and you'll be national news -- and not in a good way."

"I don't know what to say. You know about all of that?"

"Yeah, I know about all of that. You've never done a very good job of hiding it. That's why I'm so worried about you. It's way too obvious!"

The evangelist was quiet for a long time…a very long time. He stared at the floor and didn't speak; he just kind of swayed his head slowly, hypnotically back and forth, looking down all the while. Five minutes became ten minutes and then fifteen and I was starting to get concerned. The creaks and groans of the empty building hung persuasively in the air as we both sat staring at the dusty, insect-laden floor. Then, at once, he began speaking in a booming, reassuring evangelistic voice.

"Friend, I have sinned. There can be no question about that. I have succumbed to the devil's temptation and screwed many, many women though only two of them were borderline underage, I think…maybe three. I have stolen from the rich and I have stolen from the poor. I have mismanaged many of the contributions to my ministry and used much of the money to pay my mortgage and my gambling debts. I have deceived my wife and the people who believe in me. I've made horrific choices that have not only hurt me, but have hurt my relationship with God and Jesus and the sacred Mother Mary. I have no excuses – none – and am so very, very sorry for my despicable and irrational behavior. I plan to straighten myself up and 'right the ship'. First, I will get tested for any and all sexually transmitted diseases. Once I get a clean bill of health, I will pay back every cent that I have embezzled from my various entities…every cent. And I will find every urchin that I have ever ripped off and make it right with them. I can promise you that."

"I'm just looking out for you," I said. "You have a whole lot to lose and there are a whole lot of people out there who would love to make their name by taking down the likes of you. Investigative reporters, private detectives – man, those people know all the tricks."

"Maybe I deserve to get caught. Maybe that is the knock on the head that I need to straighten myself up. Hell, maybe I should call a news conference!"

"Listen to me – I *implore* you not to call a news conference. You don't need that kind of trouble – nobody does."

But he was warming to the idea. "No, maybe I really should have a news conference. Maybe I should just lay everything out on the table and let the chips fall where they may. I'm not afraid of the press. And I think that the people will forgive. They will see themselves and their frailties in me and they'll forgive. I'm convinced of it."

I tried with all my might to change his mind but the evangelist was stubborn and totally convinced that going public was the right thing for him to do at this juncture. Less than a week later, he called a news conference and was able to assemble over fifty reporters from the Dallas area and from across the nation. There were also television and radio crews present to record the happening for posterity and though I did not attend, I held my breath that things would turn out fine. They did not.

That night, all of the national newscasts showed grainy footage of the pale, sick-looking evangelist with his tragic wife by his side as he laid everything out there: The money mismanagement, the seedy dark-skinned hookers, the larceny, the affairs, the illegitimate children (which he had not mentioned to me before), the gambling, the shoplifting, the addictions, the speeding through school zones. He held nothing back. And at the end, he made the bizarre decision to quote Peter Frampton.

"Friends, I'm in you…you're in me…I'm in you…you're in me." He grabbed his wife's hand and they hurried out of the room while reporters shouted questions and humiliating accusatory statements.

Unfortunately, the resulting consequences were swift and predictably brutal. His televised ministry was summarily canceled. The Internal Revenue Service announced an immediate investigation into any and all of his financial dealings. A seemingly endless parade of women came forward with sordid details from their individual affairs with the evangelist, many producing embarrassing letters, videos and voice mail recordings. He was hit with five different demands for child support from previously silent mothers and the NAACP chastised him for his ongoing and repeated mistreatment of minorities. It was a huge national scandal, one from which he would never fully recover. The tabloids had an absolute field day and the evangelist retreated into a self-imposed and meditative seclusion.

I didn't hear from him for quite a long time. I didn't try to call him, either, because I wanted to respect his privacy, to give him some space. Finally, about a month later, I received a late night phone call and it was the evangelist and it was obvious that he had been drinking and/or drugging.

"I guess I should have listened to you, huh?"

"Listen, this isn't about who's right and who's wrong. You did what you felt you had to do. I respect that. I really do. That takes a strong man."

"I've got reporters tailing me all the time. I can't take a piss without some damn reporter sticking a microphone or camera in my face and crotch. The wife and I don't talk. The IRS is threatening me. Man, I feel crucified or some shit. This shit ain't right."

He sounded really stressed and I attempted to reassure him a bit.

"Hey, at least this all came out on *your* terms. You knew it would have come out eventually; at least this way you had *some* control."

"I had *shit* for control," he spat into the phone. "And that's the same as no control at all, OK? My life is fuckin' ruined. Friend, things will never be the same for me...*ever!*"

"And maybe that's OK," I countered. "You couldn't have gone on like you were going. You were heading down a dangerous path..."

"It's *not* OK. I loved my life. I was rich, I was famous, I was fucking anyone I wanted. Friend, you can't understand how great that is until you've been there and done that."

I was taken aback, shocked. There seemed to be no repentance, no regret except for the regret of coming forward and sharing the details about his dark side. For a supposed holy man or man of God, he seemed to really enjoy all the sinning and whatnot. I made a few perfunctory niceties and then hung up the phone, disillusioned by his raunchy and cavalier attitudes. This occasion was the last time we ever spoke live. He called a few other times but I never bothered to pick up the phone and he never bothered to leave a message.

A couple of years later, during a lazy channel surfing session, I saw the now ex-evangelist on an obscure cable home shopping network hawking collectible bibles and cell phones accessories. His delivery was as smooth as ever and he appeared pretty healthy, looking tanned and toned though having obviously gained more than a few pounds. As I watched him on the television standing there exuding chemistry with his cute co-host named Michelle Something or another, I wondered if they were doing it...or if they weren't. And if they were, was it primarily conventional or perverse? And was it meaningful or simply perfunctory?

#19

Fun With Words and Notable Theories of Heaven

I'VE NEVER ACTUALLY WORKED full-time for a daily or weekly periodical but I have spent periods of time over the years toiling on the outer fringes of the newspaper and magazine industry. I've done a bit of contract writing or "stringing" for a few local newspapers, which was basically comprised of reporting on primarily high school and college sports or other sports-related events. I've also done a few odd jobs in the industry like shooting photos, performing paste-up or layout of pages and grabbing coffee or lunch for busy, vociferous editor types. Hardcore newspaper people are a dying breed; many tend to drink heavily or abuse prescription drugs, which would seem to make their job more difficult, yet they tend to continually prevail and often excel in their line of work.

Back in the eighties and nineties, I was never surprised to pick up a newspaper or magazine and find my name in it -- not necessarily for something I wrote or did but often for something completely random of which I had no prior knowledge. Seven different times, I was listed as having accomplished a "hole-in-one" on local golf courses, including one on a par five (triple eagle?). Another time, I was listed as a witness to a double murder and was quoted as saying that the victims seemed to be "asking for it, as far as I could tell". More times than I can remember, I was listed as a survivor or life partner of someone in the obituary section. Often, I would end up being featured in articles that either criticized the police or minorities, usually taking a controversially radical point of view. None of these things ever happened; it was the work of acquaintances in the newspaper industry that were just bored and looking for a laugh or maybe two. It wasn't just *my* name they used; I would estimate that at least a quarter of the names and quotes found in newspapers and magazines back in those days were either made up or were the names of friends of the writers and editors. It was, for the most part, harmless fun and I almost always got a giggle from the fraudulent use of my identity in print.

Things did get a little hairy for me once when a writer friend wrote an article about a serial rapist and used a fabricated quote from me – identifying me as a clinical psychologist – which stated that "today's provocatively dressed women are a walking, talking advertisement for the totally understandable act of rape." I caught serious hell over that, even from people that knew me and knew that I was not a clinical psychologist. I started getting violent complaints and even death threats from strangers who considered me insensitive to the hideous crime of sexual assault. I begged my writer friend to issue some kind of retraction or correction; he said that he couldn't, that he would get fired. I didn't want him to get fired so I pretty much just took the heat and it was several months before the furor died down completely.

The only other borderline troubling incident occurred when another writer friend had authored an extremely comprehensive three-part series on the dangers of smoking. Ninety five percent of the piece detailed the documented dangers of cigarettes and tobacco and the need to outlaw the products. A tiny part of the work was dedicated to support for smoking and I was quoted as saying that "cigarettes taste good and are relaxing and I would support allowing children to at least explore the option of smoking", and that "it would seem to be a prudent thing to do". There was a good deal of public outrage over my statement; my house was egged and vandalized and I received dozens of crank calls but it did not last long and, looking back, was really not all that bad.

The other stuff was all in good fun. My name was listed in local and national election results, sports box scores, help wanted advertisements, new home listings and hard news stories about politics, interest rates, traffic accidents and boat and dock construction. It became an inside joke within my circle of friends and they enjoyed razzing me about my latest situation, whether it be about my role as a police department spokesman or my expert forecast for the country's economic growth.

The newspaper people I knew were strange birds. Most were single and the ones who were married were normally married to tall, thin women who looked like Croatians or even Fresno residents and spoke splintered English. Claude was a confirmed bachelor who always bragged about his randy bachelor pad and his seriously capped teeth. He wrote artsy editorial pieces for the sports section and loved to spend his days either in the gym or at a plaque-themed piano bar that he used to frequent. Rick was a two-toned single man who enjoyed gun ranges, Hispanic marketplaces and rumbling diesel engines. He was an associate editor with the authority to change writer's work and author catchy headlines. The bespectacled bachelor Morris had formerly worked in a high wire act and was fond of mentoring betrayed pathologists, bracing substandard structures against the weather and drinking frozen margaritas with indentured former mayors. Morris authored investigative pieces and was not very popular in the gay and lesbian community. One of the married guys was an entertainment writer named Theo who always wore the same clothes and tried to pattern his look after Jose Cuervo. He was a sanctimonious vampire wannabe who enjoyed confounding strangers by speaking in Elizabethan and bouncing good stuff off the floor.

Get these guys together in a group and there was no telling what would ensue. Sometimes it would be hilarious, sometimes it would be criminal, other times it might be profitable and/or self-defeating. Their line of work thrust them naturally into a close proximity with the troubled human element, which most likely jaded them in some ways. I had seen them burn national landmarks to the ground and I had seen them give food and money to the homeless and less fortunate. I had been present when they robbed a foreign-owned delicatessen and market and then later that same day, observed them jump-starting the car of a trembling elderly man. One day, I watched the entire group mercilessly taunt a skinny kid in a wheelchair and then immediately write him a check for $250.

There was this one deep Friday night in a bar called Opal's where the whole group plus a whole bunch more had gathered to celebrate the completion of a difficult Saturday edition. At the very same time, a gang of toughs that worshipped Sara Purcell called "The Purcell Muchachos" were carrying on in the bar and in the parking lot, shouting epithets and picking fights. The tension in the bar was palpable as the newspaper folks became increasingly irritated with the antics of the Purcell Muchachos and discussed ways to put them squarely into their place. I couldn't actually believe that they were considering fighting with these ruffians and I strongly advised them to avoid any confrontation with the Purcell Muchachos. The newspaper people totally disregarded my objections and plotted to overthrow the dangerous Purcell Muchachos with use of shocking force.

The newspaper faction numbered 33 men versus just sixteen Purcell Muchachos, which would seem to be a commanding advantage. The newspaper guys were not experienced fighters but they *were* seasoned in the art of hyperbole, which actually ended up being no help at all. Claude and Morris rallied their troops with cheers and encouragement and their group advanced to face the menacing Purcell Muchachos in the damp, dimly lit, acrid bar. The fight itself did not last long at all; the Purcell Muchachos, facing a huge manpower disadvantage, ended up walloping the newspaper guys in just a bit under three and a half minutes. It took the Fort Worth paramedics another two hours to treat the 33 unconscious men, all of whom escaped with relatively minor injuries though their egos were frightfully bruised.

I had made the conscious decision to stay out of the fray and this made many of my newspaper friends bitter. The following day, I was berated by at least a half dozen of them; they seemed to believe that if I had stepped in to lend a hand, that they would have somehow prevailed over the vastly superior and street tough Purcell Muchachos. I had no reservations about calling this "hogwash" and they promised to have some sweet revenge against me. I never knew quite why they were after me and not the Purcell Muchachos, but I imagine it was because I was an easier, weaker and maybe more centered mark.

So it was definitely not a surprise to me when my name turned up a week later in a front-page article that examined the Texas death penalty. I was quoted as having a "death list" of people that I felt deserved the Texas death penalty, including 35% of all white menopausal women, Al Roker, Phil Simms, Brandi, Nick Cage and most of the state of New Hampshire. The article went on to say that I was an oversexed activist who favored the harshest possible death for not only the people on my list, but for anyone I deemed to be ugly or slow.

Later during that same week, the Metropolitan section featured a fruity story about an undertaker accused of having sex with female corpses in the funeral home. The article quoted me as saying "I don't see anything wrong with it. I certainly don't think there's any victim here and I don't blame the undertaker for trying to have a little bit of harmless fun. People that have a problem with this are nothing but weepy fascists."

Both of these articles garnered me copious amounts of unwanted attention. There was anger amongst the masses and several prominent local ministers were calling for my head in the most obvious ways. When I was confronted directly, I attempted to explain the whole ordeal about the newspaper guys and Opal's and the Purcell Muchachos and whatnot and people looked at me like I was some kind of loon. My heartfelt, honest explanation was summarily dismissed by any and all who heard it and I was unfairly labeled as perhaps the strangest fellow in the community.

This episode in my life taught me a very hard lesson – you simply *cannot* make enemies of newspaper people because they will maliciously insert your name into weird articles that will embarrass and humiliate you. It's called the "power of the press" and its power seems to know few bounds. My name continued to periodically pop up in random articles for the next few months but eventually it all began to subside and my former newspaper buddies evidently let me off the proverbial hook. Strangely, though, I began to miss seeing my name in print and I began to crave the attention, as unfavorable as it usually tended to be. I began to consider the possibility of concocting my own outrageous utterances and observations for real and feeding them by hand to the ravenous press. It sounded like it might be fun to have some control over my own quotes and it would definitely be cool to get my name back into the spotlight, or at least back into the paper. But try as I might, I could never come up with an opinion provocative enough to get the attention of any local media personnel. The next time my name was in the newspaper was when I was listed as one of a handful of guys who lost his jeans in a bloody nationwide phone sting.

#20

. . . .

Mr. R's Friendly Good Stop

SOMETHING – STILL NOT completely sure what – compelled me to visit a filthy little convenience store called "Mr. R's Friendly Good Stop". It was located at a West Dallas intersection that I occasionally drove past but didn't dare stop, what with the gangs, hoodlums, homeless and general lamebrains hanging around the area and up a few of the trees. The parking lot was nothing but a half-acre of gravel and dust and my tires scoffed at the surface as I pulled in to park. As I got out of my car, I choked on the chalky, hovering mess that had been kicked up and my coughing seemed to apprise the neighborhood of my presence – not a good thing.

I pulled open the cracked glass door covered with beer and tobacco ads and was immediately taken aback; the place reeked of warm spices, sour perspiration and human urine and the combination was so lethal that I wanted to depart immediately but I found that I couldn't. It appeared that two men worked there – one old and one young – and they chatted cattily in a dialect I did not recognize, seemingly oblivious to my presence at that point. I craved a Mr. Goodbar and wandered up and down a couple of the aisles searching for the candy section. I wasn't all that surprised that many of the items on the shelves sported faded dirty labels covered in words from an unknown – to me – language. Some of the labels had pictures of fruit with human faces and cartoon dictators and I was having a toilsome time trying to figure out what was what.

I finally happened upon the candy section on the third aisle from the front of the store but was baffled to discover that they only had Three Musketeers – thousands of them. No Snickers, no Milky Ways, no Twix…and no Mr. Goodbars – just dusty Three Musketeers topped with what looked to be a thin film of grease or something equally as greasy. I thought it odd that the store only carried Three Musketeers bars but I really didn't mind them too much; plus, the packaging seemed intact so I grabbed a barely smashed one and headed swiftly for the checkout area.

At the counter, I placed my dollar bill flat and, using only a trembling forefinger, pushed it slowly, deliberately to the older man, who seemed to eye me with a growing skepticism. He was likely in his sixties with shiny, almost reflective gray hair, long gray sideburns that disappeared beneath the collar of his sweat-soaked shirt, lips that seemed impossibly chapped and narrow black eyes that were apparently all iris and no pupil. He had both bony, vein-filled hands on the counter in front of him and did not move them in the direction of my money.

"Are you in need of spiritual counseling?" he asked quietly.

"Nah, I'm good," I muttered, not really expecting the question.

"Where did you get that scar?" he wanted to know.

"What scar?"

"The scar on the interior of your stupidly diminished soul – I sense it. You are deeply depraved, full of delirium and other things that are bad. And the candy is $1.50."

Flustered, I clumsily fished two quarters out of my pants pocket and curtly plunked them onto the counter.

"Plus the tax," he grinned – a rotten, ghastly grin that displayed a number of unhealthy teeth and possibly organisms living within them.

"Screw the tax!" I shrieked, much like a terrified little girl, and bolted from the place, leaving the candy and my $1.50 behind. I butted my body imprudently against the entrance door, slamming it open firmly, and scurried for my car with an audience of about twenty or so toughs looking on from the sidewalk adjacent to the lot. Some were laughing, others seemed on the verge of rupture and I was in no mood to test their inclinations, hopping into my car and roaring away with squealing tires and furrowed brow.

My heart was beating at what had to be a dangerous rate as I drove down the road toward the interstate. I was relieved to be out of there, sure, but I could not rule out going back again soon. Just depends.

#21

Inspiration, Independence
and Words That Divide

THOUGH I'M NOT A professional speaker per se, I am a very enthusiastic speaker and this, combined with my relative neatness, has enabled me to be hired for a wide variety of engagements, banquets and the like. Often, a business seminar will have an agenda item to fill or club meeting will have a leftover hour to spare. I am brought in to bring "something to the table", so to speak. The organizers will give me a quick synopsis of an area they want covered and I will use my voice, hands and nuts to enrich the festivities.

It cannot be denied that I have fallen flat on a few occasions; I've been chided, booed and even chased by bat-wielding teamsters because of an ill-timed joke or limerick. But at my best, I have been…well, at my best and I mean it literally. A friendly descendant of Winslow Homer has followed me around for years and sent me a group of my most memorable quotes:

"In my estimation, the keys to success are a clear conscience, a healthy demeanor, a lawyer that won't steal from you and clothes."
 • At the combination Kip Keino family reunion/ Ted's BBQ Grand Opening in Lincoln, Nebraska.

"The last time I saw a ghost was May 29th, 2009. It was the ghost of Thomas Jefferson and he lectured me about my personal hygiene."
- At Lupercalia, to a gathered group of welders and Scandinavians.

"Double-talk got me into this fix and double-talk will get me out of it."
- To a group of 17 men at the annual "Poachers Without Borders" convention in Van Alstyne. An interesting aside is that of the 17 men, 11 were named Earl, which seemed inordinately high. The other six were Seth, Mal, Ricardo, Bert, Stan and Boz Scaggs. There was also a lady named Khloe (or Chloe).

"They say a watched pot never boils. Well, they are wrong and I can prove it!"
- To a collection of sauced troublemakers at the employee entrance to the Neiman-Marcus headquarters building on a brisk Wednesday morning.

"Yes, it was festive. That cannot be denied. But it also struck me at my very core, bringing about a gloom that rendered me utterly disconsolate. Maybe next time I'll remember to floss before dropping off at the cleaners."
- At a Mass which almost didn't make it because of the Super Bowl.

"At the end of the day, what's most important to me in life is to find things that make me think…whether they be good, bad or a little of both."
- At the Yuma Ramada to a raucous group of American tobacco growers during their annual convention/pep rally.

"TRUE GREATNESS IS NOT always obvious. Sometimes greatness is a timid little piper hiding out within a band of contemptible misfits. But when greatness is recognized, the sensation is intoxicating…kind of like wine coolers or mushrooms."
- At a banquet in Red Oak to benefit the descendants of John Phillip Sousa. The $75 per plate price tag seemed excessive but the generous helpings of salmon patties, rice and cream gravy brought about happiness. And the Sousa family beamed like Harvey Keitel at Sunday School.

"As I was reeling from a combination of bad decisions and bad luck, a silver lining appeared on the previously-murky horizon – Kentucky's Amish Buggy Bill!"

- To members of Kool and the Gang and the Platters in advance of a funeral procession for the man who invented the parfait.

"I don't have an irrational fear of insects but that doesn't mean I want 'em in my cereal."

- To attendees of Cedric the Entertainers inaugural geography camp.

"I believe it's a fundamental desire of human beings to be needed, to be a vital cog in something grand. People don't become loners by choice; they are simply unable to find a warm, comfortable place filled with smiles, hugs and acceptance – and my heart aches for them…it really does. Now who wants cake?"

- At Chuck E Cheese addressing the 14 attendees of Brandon Yarbrough's 3rd birthday party.

"I guess as children, our irrationalities seemed somehow rational."

- In the break room of a food processing plant in Sao Paulo.

"I've always found that when the night becomes a battle between good and evil, it's best to act notorious – and a little coy."

- To 31 scientists attempting to expand our horizons with bright new tools and utensils.

"If they are going to be such omnipresent figures in the lives of young people, we must ask the questions – no matter how unpleasant the answers."

- Holding court at a Stone Mountain pharmacy while waiting for more pills.

"I don't like to live in the past but I do tend to escape there occasionally, especially when the chips are down."

- To a group of Eastland, TX-based rappers on the third anniversary of their history-making turf war versus the Elks Lodge.

"People that giggle after every sentence they speak have always frightened me. I feel they are capable of inflicting more pain that I care to experience."
- To the Athens, TX swim team prior to their meet versus Mabank.

"THE GURGLING YOU HEAR below deck is my unbridled need for attention."
- To a small group of Bolivian sightseers as I captained my first cruise around Santa Cruz harbor.

"I THINK IT'S CRUCIAL for a man to act like a woman for at least an hour every day…and I mean EVERY day."
- To the entire membership of VFW Post 9095 at an after-party that served meatballs, chocolate turtles, trout and Pabst.

"TWO THINGS I ALWAYS try to avoid are urban warfare and back alley terror. By contrast, two things I am always seeking are paper mache and Hugh Beaumont memorabilia."
- In front of a gathering of about 60 clowns at the National Clown Convention in Ardmore.

"EVERY TIME I ATTEMPT to lead a purpose-driven life, I step on something sharp and subsequently overdose on Target's version of ibuprofen…every single time!"
- At the wedding of my friends from the Oubangui outstation.

"I've been completely submerged in the glitter of inclusion…twice!"
- To a cluster of prisoners including Shane, Danny, Spencer, Lonnie, Herve, Mort, Perry, The Birdman, Teddy and Uma Thurman.

"It must be a great time to be young and unconcerned with skin abnormalities."
- Addressing the audience prior to a Carlos Santana benefit concert in support of fun animals.

"I'm continually amazed by the propensity of people to jab and stick me."

- To Steph, Jill, Sondra, Autumn and the lovely ladies of Soto who were taking my picture at the Oregon State Fair.

"Often, I find myself wanting nothing more than to ease the burden of the burdened, to alleviate the suffering of the pained. But as I contemplate the notion, it becomes clear that I don't possess the ingenuity, resources or creativity to make any significant impact. I actually tried to compose a song reflective of my desire to help the helpless but it somehow transformed into a gangsta rap about turtles and their seedy little turtle caves. Much of what I do – much of what we all do – seems utterly pointless in the scheme of things. At the end of the day, I suppose it's paramount that we live and behave according to our conscience...that we adhere to what speaks to us from deep within our soul. When we find ourselves in the appropriate place and time, we'll know what to do and we'll also know how hard to press – at least I imagine so."

- To about three dozen attendees of an "Edgar Allan Poe-fest" in Alexandria, Louisiana.

"CONTRARY TO POPULAR BELIEF, the key to happiness is not always found within; sometimes it lies in a mortally-flawed tub at the end of the highness."

- To six board-certified surgeons as they prepped for work on one of the governors.

I reckon I've done over 6000 of these speaking engagements, some important, some frivolous and others just plain spurious. In good times I've been poetic and prophetic while at other times I've been incoherent, uncouth and even stinking. It's not always possible for me to predict when I'll be "on" but it does seem that I perform better when they feed me something sweet – or when they offer a massage under the lights.

#22

The Mother of Aggression

I THOUGHT IT HAD to be a mistake when I received a Valentines card in the mail from television heart throb Katie Couric. We really didn't know each other that well; sure, we'd both been guests at a couple of the same parties, one in Hollywood and the other in Nocona, but we'd spoken only briefly and I never sensed a truly strong bond. We knew a few of the same people and we shared a weird fascination with weed killer but I didn't see a strong foundation for a real friendship. Evidently, she saw things differently.

The card she sent expressed that she wanted me to "be" her Valentine and that her love for me was "endless, fragrant and fruitful". Katie's handwritten note explained that she could not get my fingernails off her mind and that she believed that I possessed quite a bit of the "right stuff". She ended the note by saying that we should do some serious dating together and that I would not be sorry if I were to pop a preemptive dating question. As confused as I was, I was also intrigued and wondered what it would be like to date Katie Couric in a situation where we could discuss my fingernails and weed killer in relative quiet and privacy.

Katie called the next day to say that she would be in town soon and wanted to go on a date with me to the kind of place that could augment the experience in untold ways. I asked her exactly when she would be in town and she replied that she was already jetting my way and that she had come down with a minor case of the jitters. Katie Couric was a huge catch, in my estimation; she was a real cutie and looked good in all the right areas. And her profound intelligence was stimulating without being at all intimidating.

Five hours later, this woman that had to be Katie Couric was at my front door. We embraced in the doorway for nearly 45 minutes and I thought that she smelled and felt good...good, indeed. She was much shorter than me and as we hugged, her breasts and my crotch seemed to intermingle like two peas in a pod. It was one of those moments in life that you pray will never end, yet you also find yourself ready to move on, to get on with it.

"I've missed you so! Katie growled seductively. "You've been on my mind constantly!"

"I'm flattered, Katie. I'm a little shocked that I made that kind of impact. I mean, we only spoke for a few minutes in Nocona and I think only seven or eight words in Hollywood."

"Nonsense!" she said. "You floored me...you really did. Since we met, nothing has been the same for me. Food tastes different. Wine tastes different. Clothes fit differently. Jakob Dylan sounds different. My life has changed for the better and I have you to thank for it."

"But Katie, you already had so much going for you. You were famous and damn good at your job. And so damn hot...how could someone like me have such an impact on someone like you?"

"It's your nose, silly. I first noticed it in Nocona and recognized it again immediately in Hollywood. It's beautiful. It makes me feel better about myself and it lifts the spirits of everyone in the room. It's regal and astonishing in its own way. I think I love it. Or I'm *in* love with it."

Now *I* was floored. This woman that had to be Katie Couric was in love with me...or at least she was in love with my nose. I invited her into my cozy home and after slight hesitation, she accepted. We sat cross-legged on a rug in my living room floor, chanting the poetry of Tom Mackin and making understandable barfing noises. She asked me to consider amputating my own damn pinkie finger and I replied that it wasn't a rational thing to do. We told each other our deepest, darkest secrets and shared our grandest dreams about life, love, kites and weed killer. Katie stayed for hours and I don't remember her blinking even once.

When bedtime rolled around, I asked Katie what her plans were for the *very* near future. She lifted her eyebrows indignantly.

"Don't expect me to share your bed. That idea blows and I'm not sleeping with that," she said, gesturing toward the general area of my crotch.

"I don't expect you to, Katie. That's not what we're about, is it? Our relationship is about trust and jewelry and all things precious."

"Trust, I agree with. I don't think our relationship has much to do about jewelry, though. Pretense is a tool for insolvent people...not us."

Katie Couric spent the night at my house but refused to share my bed, which was fine. We spent most of the time reading aloud from a dictionary with me in the bed and Katie lying on the floor nearby. We both loved reading the dictionary and felt empowered by the new words that we learned. I dared her to work the word "sarcophagus" into a future newscast and she urged me to fight temptation at every turn. Sometime around 3am, I dozed off only to awaken at 7am with Katie Couric in my kitchen preparing me a four-course breakfast.

There can be no question that Katie Couric was sending me mixed signals. She had spent the night in my house but had not allowed me to insert my parts anywhere important. She had shared of herself and confided dark secrets yet had remained guarded and even standoffish. Katie was a well-known and highly touted professional woman yet here she stood barefoot in my kitchen throwing together an appealing breakfast for two. It was unfortunate that she lost a nail in one of the omelets but I ended up crunching it with my molars along with the ham and peppers and whatnot.

I took Katie Couric to see the Texas Schoolbook Depository and Southfork Ranch that day, both of which fascinated her. We had lunch at a Whataburger and got flavored coffee at this gas station that was often a hangout of mine. The clerk there was called "Isabel" and she was a limber Puerto Rican Haitian with one eyebrow and chronic hangnails. She took an immediate liking to Katie and showed her a photo album full of ultrasounds and yogurt recipes. I don't know how Katie truly felt about Isabel but she acted nice, friendly and affected. The two chatted about ugly neckties and the peculiarities of the Amish while engaging in a friendly game of checkers on top of a wobbly cracker barrel. We left the gas station and headed to the sprawling Mary Kay Headquarters because Katie was anxious to take the daily tour. However, we found ourselves unable to enter the building. It was being guarded by a local gang of ruffians called "Cinco Mas" that used intimidation tactics and chains to keep folks like us the hell away.

Our day concluded with pie at a hot dog eating contest on the grounds of Texas Instruments. Katie used the occasion to inform me that she planned to propose to Prince Harry on the deck of a vast yacht in the Indian Ocean in just a couple of weeks. I was totally shocked – I felt that we had bonded and that we might have a future together. Her Prince Harry admission was a monumental setback in our relationship; still, I felt that if I could somehow bed her, that I would be able to win her over with my technique. We returned to my home that night and once inside my house, I slung Katie up over my shoulder and attempted to carry her to my bed so that I might bed her. She wriggled free and we both sort of tumbled to the carpeted floor underneath a silver painting of a smiling fish.

"How dare you!" Katie shrieked, shaking with tenacity, I guess. "I can never sleep with you. My body belongs to Harry. You, of all, people should know that! You, of all, people should *understand*! Sometimes you're such a disappointment!"

"Come on, Katie. You're like three times his age. He's not going to marry you. He doesn't love you. He'll never love you."

"None of this concerns you," she replied dismissively. "This is between Harry and me and no one else." She removed some apparatus and a little kit from her handbag and began rolling an oversized doobie.

"Katie Couric...sometimes in life you have to seize the moment. You have to take the bull by the horns. We're both here. I have a penis and you have a vagina. It seems almost stupid not to take advantage of our situation."

"That's the difference between you and me," she said. "As much as I love your nose, I have no desire to dive into your bed with you and roll around like maniacs on meth. As Shakespeare would say, 'The rattlesnake around my neck keeps my brain from smelling like generosity until I am tranquilized behind an Arby's'."

"OK...well, that doesn't sound like Shakespeare to me but I'm not going to force you into something you're not comfortable with. I guess you can just sleep down there on the floor again tonight and we'll keep our things from doing any freakish mingling."

Katie and I slept separately again that night and when I awoke the next morning, she was doing some yoga moves or something to a soundtrack of what sounded like pure evil while wearing an unseemly one-piece leotard. I knew immediately she would be leaving for good that day and my emotions were decidedly mixed. Of course I was going to miss her. She had won me over, undoubtedly with her eclectic mix of sweet, sour and the other. But I was also certain that the time had come for her to execute a graceful exit from my life in more ways than just the one.

I loaded Katie and her cosmetic bag full of mementos into my car and proceeded to drive her to the main airport. We rode in mainly a thick silence, with just a few assorted sighs, coughs, sniffs and grunts reverberating off the inside walls of my vehicle. I think we were both somewhat bitter at the way things had turned out but, at the same time, we were both slightly coy and playing a little "hard to get" for most of the ride. We drove into the airport property and I pulled the car to the front of the bustling American Airlines terminal. I stopped and we both sat wordless, staring straight ahead for almost five straight minutes. I was becoming very fidgety and uncomfortable until Katie broke the silence with a bombshell.

"You're a tall and wonderful man and I can't deceive you any longer. I have done you terribly wrong and all I can ask is that you consider forgiveness. I am not Katie Couric, the evening network news anchor. I know I look like her and I get that all the time. My name *is* Katie, but I am Katie, the granddaughter of Muriel Petrie, a prominent Hollywood stylist and confidant from the forties. My grandmother had many fine qualities but, unfortunately, she also instilled in all of us the virtues of lies and deception. I am not proud of my depressing lifestyle; as a matter of fact, it downright sickens me. But I have been unable to effect a substantial change in the way I lead my life and the byproduct of this is that I hurt nice people. I'm so sorry…so very sorry."

"Fine!" Without a second of hesitation, I jumped out of the car and rushed around to the passenger side. I yanked opened the door, grabbed Katie by the arm and pulled her surely and sternly out of my car. I reached into the backseat and grabbed her stuffed bag, tossing it onto the concrete walkway and spilling mementos (including a boogie board and a warm gun) haphazardly here and there about the place. I stalked back around to the driver's side, got in and sped away with genuine conviction, never turning to look back even once.

While driving back home, I noticed a colorful billboard that had never caught my attention before even though I drove this particular highway quite often. The billboard was an advertisement for a company that sells spas and hot tubs and featured a woman that looked like the singer Gloria Estefan wearing a one-piece bathing suit and reclined in a hot tub laughing at some unseen, unheard joke with her feet sticking up carelessly out of the water. The left foot looked completely normal – maybe a little small. The right foot was missing two toes and appeared to be three sizes larger than the left. It also sported a gaudy tattoo of a smashed bird on the sole and the heel seemed to be plagued with spurs – real goddamn spurs.

As disconcerting as this sight was, it also made me feel the urge to extend an unconditional forgiveness to the departed Katie. And so I did, but only in my freaking head.

#23

Activism and Popcorn Chicken in a Box

I REMEMBER HEARING SOME conservative blowhard on the radio one afternoon lamenting what he called "nutty" activists who were so keenly obsessed with the rights of animals that they actually valued animal lives more than human lives. These folks considered it sinful to eat animals or to use them to create clothing or shelter. The blowhard thought this notion to be absurd since animals were out there in the animal kingdom absolutely tearing each other to shreds anyway – so why should people feel bad about tearing them to shreds when given the opportunity, whether it be for constructive use or for sport. I found myself in agreement with the blowhard on this; I've watched nature shows which filmed lions and tigers and cheetahs trapping and greedily devouring zebras and gazelles and wildebeest. In some of these same shows, Great White Sharks chewed the hell out of seals, and crocodiles bit the hell out of birds and even horses in some cases.

I think predatory animals are nothing but big bullies and outright jerks. They prey on the small and the weak and the helpless and yet some people worship these menaces and even set up nature reserves to house, feed and protect them. I think they deserve to be stalked and chased and then consumed while still living. Sometimes, I think it would be cool to take an axe and bury it into the rear end of a Bengal tiger or use my hands to forcibly extract an eye from a hammerhead shark. Payback can often be a bitch and some of these bullying animals seem to have a shit load of payback owed to them.

I eventually made the decision to become affiliated with a group called "PAFBA" (People Against Fuckin' Bully Animals). The organization was created by a congenial guy called "Bud" – nobody seemed to know his full name – and had "swollen" to a total membership of 63 people by the time I got myself involved. There were membership dues and weekly meetings that featured an agenda and a spread consisting of shark meat, crackers and boiled lion mane. PAFBA had a monthly newsletter which was a cool Microsoft Word-based ditty printed on recycled paper made from dry leaves and thyme.

Some of the PAFBA board members were real pieces of work. Bud's right-hand man was a presidential-looking sort called Owen. By day, Owen managed an office full of thick, middle-aged women with large hairdos who processed claims and researched Civil War myths and hymns. But his nights belonged to PAFBA and Owen was fastidious in organizing the meeting agendas and in aggressively recruiting any white males over the age of twelve. Owen was married to a woman nine years his senior and the couple owned a couple of adopted Japanese kids.

The PAFBA treasurer was an unemployed, hairy auto mechanic named Reid. Reid was a former collegiate basketball star who never quite adjusted to life out of the media spotlight. Reid had lead his team to college basketball's Final Four but, alas, he was a slow white kid with decent ball-handling skills and the quickness of deep-fried scalp and thus had absolutely no future in professional basketball. He was a bachelor who could no longer get the beautiful people to perform sex acts on him and he seemed to live the pathetic life of a lonely aging hipster. Reid signed autographs for people even though they didn't ask and always wore white suede shoes whenever he felt stressed or sick to his stomach.

The Sergeant-at-Arms was well-known local activist named Truman Capote (not the writer). Truman was fanatical in his hatred for predatory animals and his spacious home was filled with all kinds of dead lions, tigers, bears and whatnot that were stuffed and posed in threatening postures. Truman loved to punch the animals and burn them with lighted cigarettes while performing his duties as an astute kung fu master in one of the dimly lit stairwells. He enjoyed hanging crepe paper streamers from the animal's tails and found himself consuming far too much ice cream cake in their damn presence.

Bud, Owen, Reid and Truman spent their time together examining the narcissism of lions and the hatefulness of Great White Sharks and their offspring. They enjoyed drinking aged booze, snorting powdered coke and commentating on frame-by-frame predatory attack footage that flickered monotonously in glorious black and white from the semi-faulty projector. Sometimes they sat in relative silence, somberly observing the action and then making rather astute comments about the scenes of carnage. Other times, they giggled like schoolgirls in heat and playfully cackled and tossed iron and things about.

One of history's saddest days was the day that the little PAFBA office space was raided by some ambitious federal authorities with nothing better to do. The rumor was that they had been tipped off by an impassioned sitcom star who had evidently been wronged by one of the PAFBA board members during a marathon poker game in or around a bed and breakfast in Jefferson, Texas. The agents stormed the offices on a stormy Monday morning and absolutely trashed the place in true textbook fashion. They used axes to destroy desks and chairs, tossed files around like hepatitis, spread feces on the walls and into tiny crevices and set fire to a few unarmed and unnamed creatures. The agents collected inflammatory evidence against the PAFBA organization and its subsidiaries and, in an intriguing turn of events, began to recruit people to eliminate Bud, Owen, Reid and Truman in extreme painful fashion. It may not have been normal procedure for federal authorities to plot murder against citizens but this did not hinder their zeal for the endeavor. In no time, they were placing newspaper advertisements and filming television commercials soliciting shady folks to do the terrible deed and offering generous cash payments along with a 401K plan.

The ensuing bad publicity and media scrutiny doomed PAFBA and I was not at all happy about it. I had found comfort there; it gave me a feeling of belonging that I was able to find in no other place. These people, their beliefs and their extraordinary quirks appealed to me in almost indefinable ways. I enjoyed their intellect and their spirited manner as well as the rapid-fire banter. They were also very clean and they kept all of their things extremely organized and carefully stacked. The entire group was very good about keeping their genitals put away and ensuring that the areas around their genitals were well kempt and free of tangles. The PAFBA meetings and events were highlights for me and I always found myself looking forward to them and rehearsing small talk scenarios while holding and massaging empty tumblers in my kitchen.

Bud and Owen ended up murdered by some white trash whatnot and Reid and Truman definitely got the message, dropping forever out of sight. The murders had been cruel and painful affairs for Bud and Owen; they had lost tons of blood and been embarrassed in front of an agile crew filming a television commercial for dandruff shampoo. The details were revealed worldwide and I found them painful to consider. When the funerals were conducted, I stayed home because I just could not bear to go; it was just too difficult. I was told later that the pallbearers were actors and actresses from the cast of "The Days and Nights of Molly Dodd" and that some were attractively built. The eulogies for Bud and Owen lasted a combined 623 words and the crying that occurred in the church came from some kind of game and nothing else – at least that's what I was told.

I never lost my hatred for predatory animals or my love for the Texas landscape. Often when intoxicated, I would try to make friends by planting things along the desolate highways when no one was looking. After all the planting, I would hand paint murals in the pastures that overlooked steamy villages cloaked in fog or something similar. Of course, I was doing it for Bud, Owen, Reid and Truman but when the villagers chose not to jeer, I knew that they had also benefited immensely from my generous activity. I turned down Letterman, Conan and McEnroe in short order but finally relented to questioning when Nancy Travis came calling in a skimpy two-piece swimsuit cut down to there. She asked specifically about Bud's dietary habits and the scientific cause of guitar feedback on records from the sixties and seventies. I took off my reflective sunglasses and proceeded to lecture her about things such as mojo, insanity, spittle, geriatric programming and eventually the Tropic of Capricorn. She giggled, which sent me into a laughing fit that I could not contain without my medication. When the interview aired on the cable news, it was edited in such a way as to depict me as a wholly concentrated mass of envy. This nearly forced me off the deep end though, thankfully, not quite.

I'll never forget the special feeling I derived from my involvement with PAFBA and its subsidiaries. I often think about it, especially when I'm wearing a mask or hankering for a flavored Twinkie from some obnoxious store clerk. I sometimes wonder about Reid and Truman and what they might be up to in terms of backwards aggression. I feel like PAFBA is probably dead but I also think it would be pretty easy to revive, especially with the support of a core of ex-members and maybe a graying federal judge or two. Of course, this prospect became somewhat problematic when Dateline ran an expose over a series of nights and proclaimed PAFBA "nothing but a dang ole dump of Nazi garbage at the stroke of midnight". The public outcry was akin to what was heard when the French won the 1998 World Cup and many people were placed into custody as well as jeopardy.

I've always considered murder to be troubling and when murders began to occur in the wake of PAFBA, it made me sad. With all the murders going on in the animal kingdom, I really hated the thought of people killing people known to me in our supposedly civilized society. And though I was saddened, I was even more determined than ever to correct what I deemed to be abhorrent behavior by goddamn suspects and twisted individuals. Locating a stable platform in a makeshift doorway, I took a deep drag from something pungent and delivered a gripping diatribe on the evils of killing living stuff and that this particular sin tends to be unforgivable. A few of the masses took notice but not nearly enough and I soon became convinced to withdraw from the public eye and dispose of my PAFBA obsession once and for all. At this point, I decided it would be prudent to find a hobby and I began building rickety time machines out of used chopsticks utilizing only my right hand. It was fun and it gave me the lift I needed at that point in my life…it really did.

#24

• • • • • • • • • • • • • • • • • • •

Pills and the Pleasure of Oblivion

MY PAINS, REAL AND imagined, have grown with frightening regularity as I have aged. When I was young, a bruise, a cut or even a broken something came and went quickly and with very little trouble. As the years passed, however, every morning became an inwardly brutal, often fruitless struggle with headaches, knee pain, backaches, eye pain, ear pain, tongue pain, nose pain and sore ankles and feet. I just don't understand why a night's sleep brings all of this pain bubbling to the surface and why in the morning I feel like some kind of elementary school science experiment gone horribly awry. It makes no sense and I don't get it at all. An arrow-straight licensed doctor with an office once told me that it had something to do with a Full Moon effect and someone's dirty habits but I'm not buying that curious load of rubbish.

"How can a Full Moon and someone's dirty habits cause me to have pain in the morning?"

"You're not understanding me," the doctor said. "Those things don't *cause* you to have pain. Those things *are* your pain."

"Huh?"

"You're just confused. When you break down your pain into geographical arenas, you'll find that connecting the dots will bring you more relief than you ever imagined possible. That and pills."

Connecting the dots didn't work out that well but the pills certainly did. It was what I had been searching for all of my life! With pills, my pain was virtually eliminated and a soft, lazy feeling of "well being" sloshed about in my stomach and brain until the effect wore the hell off. And when the effect wore off, I downed another pill or two and enjoyed a feeling of renewed "well being", basking in the glory of a painless and fuzzy altitude.

I can never forget the night a dozen years ago when, after an evening chock full of Nigerian sake and poorly disguised horsemeat, I took a terrible tumble in a gloomy parking lot which resulted in a piece of fibula sticking through my skin and whatnot. The pain was worse than the sake and things were not looking very good for me until my emergency room trip resulted in a bottle of thirty or so pills. The pills were so good that I plum forgot the ankle and I spent the next few days floating on a cloud of pill-induced euphoric stupor that resulted in my first teary-eyed acceptance of a higher power or something.

My problem was that in the beginning, I was not very good at conserving my pill supply. Whenever I got hurt, I obtained some but I always went through them far too quickly. What I needed was a friendly doctor to supply my pill requirements in plentiful enough quantities so that conservation would not be problematic. Doctors like this do not grow on trees...but they do exist. I found two of them – one from Desoto and the other from Pantego. The Desoto doctor was a little feminine tart who was actually a biological male with a beard and a penis. The doctor from Pantego was a little league baseball manager who wore saggy pants like a thug from the tough neighborhood to the south.

These two doctors supplied me with pills whenever I wanted and didn't ask for much at all in return. The Desoto doctor only wanted my discarded nail clippings while the Pantego doctor asked for me to teach him horseshoes. I was really lucky because the street level dealers wanted up to $25 per pill and if I had been forced to pay that amount, my high forehead would have seriously creased from the depression -- and emphatically so.

On my third trip to the Desoto doctor, he began to express a bit of motherly concern over my increasing dependence.

"Don't you think you ought to slow down a bit?" he asked.

"No. Why?"

"Well, it seems to me that your body is beginning to develop immunity to the medication and this can't be good for you. It's going to take more and more of the pills to get to the feeling that you desire.

This can result in a whole host of health issues, if you allow it to. I know this because I'm a doctor."

"Doc, I think I'm fine. The pills are really just a habit for me. I don't need to have them – it's just something I'm used to doing. Sometimes I just tuck them under my tongue for the hell of it...to know they're there. The pills make me the kind of person I always thought I should be."

"OK. As long as you have it under control..."

"Don't worry."

The Pantego doctor never expressed any concern at all. I told him how many I wanted and he wrote out the prescription. In retrospect, I realize that he was going through marital problems and had gotten into some kind of physical relationship with the television character known as "Screech". These factors likely clouded his judgment in his professional dealings with me and his other patients. One of his other patients – a bakery manager named Erica – had been getting Prozac and medicinal marijuana from him for years even though she confided in me that the only thing wrong with her was a distorted fashion sense. Another – a former major league baseball player – was the recipient of all the Accutane he could ingest. For most people, Accutane had no pleasurable effect but for this guy, it provided him the equivalent of a crack-based orgasmic excretion.

My daily pill usage peaked at around twenty per day in the middle of a rock-hard and foggy November. Though my speech was essentially slurred, I felt great all of the time and was mostly able to walk a straight line without any assistance. I was not aware of any serious side effects but, looking back, it seems conceivable that my liver may have been compromised and my kidneys were probably systematically siphoned. Despite this, I felt an imperial peace in my brain that seemed to impossibly straddle two distinct halves of an impartial and untainted cycle.

For me, rock bottom occurred in a Shreveport casino on a surprisingly cool Tuesday night in July. I was sitting at a blackjack table playing hand after hand, comforted by more than my usual amount of pills, mixed with the overt generosity of free as hell cocktails. I started doing everything wrong, standing on seven, hitting soft nineteen, doubling down on twenty. The other players at the table were getting mad and dealers and pit bosses were snickering. I felt humiliated and began challenging everyone to fights and whatnot. Then I jumped on top of the blackjack table and proclaimed myself to be Rick Astley while thumping my chest like a Russian ice cream man. Security began gathering and I jumped from table to table, stomping on playing cards and breaking one of the roulette wheels with an ill-timed step or stomp.

The casinos in Shreveport are all on riverboats and I found my way to an outside deck and dove headfirst into the Red River. I swam the river for miles, through downtown, across Cross Lake and soon into Texas. I eventually trudged out of the river and found a place on shore to take a nap – a little snooze that ended up lasting almost two full days. I was eventually startled awake by the sound of a coyote chewing on a live rabbit and soon made my way to the nearest highway and was able to hitchhike back to my hometown.

Once I completed the math, I was disgusted to find that I had lost over three thousand dollars in that damn casino. Not only had I squandered the original thousand that I took with me, but I had also made five subsequent trips to the all-too-convenient ATM and managed to lose every single dollar that had been extracted from the device. I was physically sick of myself and sick of my abhorrent way of dealing with the living. The pills had turned me into someone I didn't know, someone who had lost his fucking way. I decided then and there that I had to quit the pills and figure out the best way to live my life without them.

For my detoxification effort, I enlisted the help of a dog-training outfit that advertised on all of the cable outlets and radio stations. Of course, I wasn't a dog but I honestly felt that many of the same factors that were critical in successful dog training would be essential in enabling me to rid myself of the dastardly curse. And it worked – to a degree. The dog trainers and some of their mates basically camped in my foyer and immediately handled any of the nasty side effects as they arose. They wrote slogans for my madness and skillfully cleaned up the messes that tended to turn up at the most inopportune times. They time-stamped my forehead when meals ran late and basically shoveled away whatever ailed me.

The major downside to this method was the ferocity with which they withheld the pills. I was beaten to a goddamn pulp on at least five different occasions and was verbally assaulted more times than I care to remember. I was taunted for my shortcomings and was called names that I would not call an animal. I was denied food and my sneakers were intentionally laced with aggressive, improper fungus. My family was continually threatened and a silly little church I was rumored to have once attended ended up burned to the ground in a brazen case of prophetic arson. The mental and physical torture gradually weakened my resistance and after a month or so, I found myself no longer in need of the pills. The dog trainers unceremoniously flushed my remaining stash down the toilet and I stood at attention and flashed a grateful two-fingered salute as they completed the deed.

Finally clean and rid of my dark addiction, I set out to make my peace with the world at large. My first stop was a local synagogue that had been profiled in a television news piece because of their surfing rabbi. I found this very rabbi in a comfy office lined with lanyards and made my intentions clear.

"I've just traveled here from the black depths of the devil's bosom. I come here on a mission to flood this world with my newly discovered confidence. I need to understand the circumference of your immunity."

"I have no idea what you're talking about."

"I saw you on the television. I thought, of all people, you would understand my ordeal. I thought you could offer some insight and maybe a bit of helpful advice."

"Young man, I am a rabbi. I'm not some insipid excuse for a super hero. I attempt to educate my followers in the ways of God and even Jesus, to a certain extent. I'm not sure who you think I am...but I'm not him."

I know I was crestfallen at this point. After seeing this guy on television, I just *knew* he had some answers for me. Instead, he was a huge disappointment, as was the entire Jewish religion. I wasn't Jewish, but I had always felt a certain kinship with the Jewish people and their employees. After this encounter with the rabbi, I lost most of my respect for Judaism and many of its subsidiaries. I was conflicted and I was having trouble figuring out where to turn and what to do about my precarious condition, which seemed inclined to deteriorate at any moment.

Basically, pills were now out of my life, leaving in their wake a huge void to fill. Without the pills to caress and eventually pop, I discovered too much time on my hands and too few things to give me pleasure. I'm not trying to be crude or anything, but pleasure is one of the four elements that living beings pursue with little regard for consequences. Without the possibility of pleasure, life would definitely lose much of its luster – no question about it. My pursuit of pleasure at this point began to involve Monopoly, stagehands, the Platt Amendment and skimboards. Initially, nothing measured up to the pills. Eventually, however, pleasure began to fly at me in many forms and the pills became nothing more than a memory to me.

A postscript to my pill experience is that I later became helplessly addicted to nasal spray. It began during a bout with the flu and continued for well over a year, as I found myself unable to function in society without a spray bottle of nasal medication ready in my front pocket at all times. I was constantly stuffy and unable to breathe without it and it became the actual meaning in my life. I even made up a little poem about nasal spray that went like this:

With my nasal spray, I share a love,
A love that makes my life seem nice.
When I sniff it into my cranial cavity
And feel the sting of the smarmy effect,
I feel like a bug in a Vegas hotel
With the brows trimmed to a hideous degree.

I was eventually able to kick this new addiction with the help of Coke Zero, a box of syringes and a tiny hypnotist named Cliff, who was able to convey to me that nasal spray was petty, immaterial and without merit. Cliff (who had twelve children) provided me with a mantra and a bedpan to combat the impulse and handed me a crisp one hundred dollar bill when my treatment was complete. He was really very cool, though not very tall at all.

#25

. · · · · · · · · · · · · · · · · · · ·

Nail Salons and Hitting Below the Belt

IT WAS HUMBLING, TO say the least. When I strolled into the quaint little nail salon and requested assistance from the nearest technician for some pressing issues with my fingernails, she took one hasty glance and immediately threw both hands up in front of her face, exclaiming, "No way, Jose!" while contorting her chubby face into the shape of a battery or fruit.

Frantic and in need, I endeavored to plead my case to the haughty and stubborn nail technician.

"Listen, this is a nail salon. It says so on your sign out front. I've got some obvious problems with my nails and I need your help. I'll pay whatever you charge for this service. I just need this fixed. I have pain and there is the embarrassment that goes with it. Can you help me? Please?"

Her nametag read "Sheryl" and she just shook her head doggedly. Her curly red hair seemed to lag behind the rest of her head as it wagged left...right...left...right. She stood with chubby hands posted on wide, child-bearing hips and appeared to be immovable on the subject.

"You go now!"

"But Sheryl..."

"Out now! Don't make me call the cops!"

Forlorn, defeated and increasingly unkempt, I turned to leave. I pushed open the glass door and headed out into the mist, the chirping chime of the door alarm echoing with bittersweet opulence in my good ear. I gazed somberly back over my shoulder and took note of the capacious, brightly-lit "Welcome" sign, complete with a grinning cartoon Billy goat smoking what appeared to be a real cigar. Welcome? Evidently not if your fingernails are packed with embedded shards of glass and stained by nine distinct types of tree sap. Nope, they definitely don't welcome; they cruelly kick you to the outside and don't care at all that you are in discomfort or something worse. I imagined that Sheryl and the other nail technicians were inside having a hearty laugh at my expense, mocking my plight and likely wishing me injury in my spine.

What Sheryl and her coworkers neglected to recognize was that I was a moral, reputable human being with family, friends and loved ones who genuinely cared for me. These people worried for me when I was troubled and they celebrated with me when I triumphed or achieved. They showered me with unqualified loyalty and were always there for me when I found myself in need. I doubt that Sheryl had any friends that she could talk to when she was lacking something crucial. I'm sure that Sheryl's family had practically disowned her because of her obnoxiousness, vileness and total lack of moral standards in almost every situation. Yes, that Sheryl was a pitiable, wretched soul who deserved nothing less than a racking, arduous death in a painfully public setting. And she was far too big.

I made it out to my car, paused for a brief interlude, and then left my car behind, trudging out into the misty darkness, searching for something or someone nice in a spooky Arkadelphia night.

#26

● ● ● ● ● ● ● ● ● ● ● ● ● ● ● ● ● ● ● ●

The Relative Heartbreak of Psoriasis

AS MUCH AS I am reluctant to admit it, I experienced the heartbreak of psoriasis first-hand and I can tell you that it was not fun and also pretty damn sad. Evidently, I was endowed with active and precocious T-cells, which resulted in psoriasis of the arm, back and especially the fingernails. I first noticed the disease as a teenager and in those emotionally formative years, psoriasis is the *last* thing you want to be contending with. I had a high school girlfriend who discovered an outbreak of psoriasis on my lower back while attempting to burrow her tongue into some place nice. She screamed and jumped out of bed, throwing on her clothes and figuratively cutting to black.

Kids can be cruel but some were more accepting of the disease than others. The cartoonist for the student newspaper created an editorial cartoon that, in essence, praised my psoriasis-stricken fingernails for their courage and their cuddly demeanor. He called my fingernails an "inspiration" and "definitely worth the price of admission". Shortly after publication of that cartoon, my fingernails were actually named as the class' "Most Likely to Succeed". Additionally, my fingernails got a date with Rhonda Davis -- the hottest girl in school -- and though the date ended with something being indoctrinated with metal horns, it was still a quite impressive feat.

The downside of psoriasis was as debilitating as it was humiliating. Not only was I taunted by many of the other kids, but I also found myself being taunted by teachers, librarians, truck drivers and even their pets. The cruelty was man-made and gargantuan; I was often reduced to tears by the searing barbs and the fierce, unrelenting smirks. Some people did not seem to understand that *psoriasis was an affliction*! It wasn't poor hygiene and it wasn't bad manners – it was something over which I had no fuckin' control and it kept me from having a fully functional home office – I know that much for certain.

I was always pretty happy about the fact that the psoriasis stayed confined to lower back, arms and fingernails. I feared that, at some point, it would spread to my penis and throughout the groin area, which would have been uncomfortable for my potential sexual partners. Despite this bit of positive news, psoriasis was no cakewalk and the suffering that I experienced was borderline insane – insane like the dickens.

There was the time when I was processing a bank transaction at the last possible minute and my arm psoriasis had flared like there was no tomorrow. Though psoriasis is not contagious, the cute little teller shrieked with passion and sprinted straight out of the bank and, I believe, to her car to drive home. The other bank employees assumed that there must be a robbery in progress and I was summarily wrestled to the ground, hogtied and forced to inhale toluene. When the police arrived, they manhandled me with excessive force and escorted me outside to answer their questions or something.

"Why the hell are you robbing this bank?"

"I'm not robbing anything. I came to make a deposit. Look – my deposit slip and a check are in my front shirt pocket."

"We know you're up to no good. That teller was definitely screaming about something. What was your plan? Who are your accomplices?"

"I have no plan and I have no accomplices. You want to know what she was screaming about? Take a good look at my right arm. Go ahead!"

The group of cops all leaned over to inspect the psoriasis that was having its way with my right arm.

"Oh my God," whispered one.

"Jesus H. Christ!" exclaimed another.

Two of the cops immediately leaned over and began vomiting all over the sidewalk in front of the bank. This caused a bit of a chain reaction and before I knew it, there were a dozen people – cops and passerbys – puking all around the area by the bank and a nearby video store. Did I feel responsible? Reluctantly, yes. Of course I wasn't robbing the bank but my hideous skin and aggressive T-cells had brought about uncomfortable and even painful moments for a host of innocent people. I wanted to do something to help but I could not even hold back their hair while they vomited because I was freaking handcuffed. All I could really do was make sympathetic faces and supportive utterances while folks went through their personal hells and ruined some pretty nice clothes in the process. I was eventually released and cleared of all charges – but I was also branded with a stern stamp of semi-permanent non-inclusion.

Another time, my psoriasis got the better of me was at what was supposed to be a charitable event. I was manning a command center in a shopping center parking lot collecting blankets and winter wear for the homeless and otherwise disadvantaged. I felt good about donating my time to this cause and I summoned as much enthusiasm as possible while soliciting the goods from the various donors. Clothing concealed the psoriasis on my arm and back but my fingernail psoriasis ended up exposed for all to see and judge.

Most of the day passed uneventfully and I found myself accumulating a huge pile of stuff that would be helpful to those in need. But when an El Camino full of teenage boys pulled up to the site, I sensed that there might be trouble in the offing. There were five of them in all and though they were swigging sodas and smoking cigarettes, their skin was absolutely flawless. I guess I was somewhat impressed that they were donating to such a good cause but was soon disappointed to find that what they were donating was a half-empty box of condoms.

"Guys, this is not really what we're looking for. We're hoping to collect blankets and clothing to keep the homeless people warm. Do you have anything like that?"

"Shit no, dude," the driver said. "We thought we'd give some condoms so that when the street people screw, they wouldn't be making any ugly babies…cuz all street people are ugly…right?"

All of the kids in the car shouted out their agreement with a rousing chorus of "hell yeahs" and "right ons". I was disgusted by their cockiness but made every attempt to keep my wits about me.

"Hey fellas, do you guys realize that Ally Sheedy used to be homeless? You don't think she's ugly, do you?" I didn't know if this was true or not – in fact, I'm reasonably sure that it wasn't true. But the words just came out and sounded pretty good and fitting at that point.

"For real? Are you shittin' us?"

"No shit guys." I was absent-mindedly fiddling with my buttons when one of the teens in the backseat noticed by psoriasis-engulfed nails.

"What the fuck is that? What the fuck is that on your fingers?"

I tried to casually glance down at my hand. "Oh, it's nothing -- just a little leftover psoriasis from my last outbreak...nothing to worry about."

"Like hell!" the driver said as he jumped out of the car. The four other teenagers followed his lead and it wasn't long before they were beating me like the proverbial drum. I wasn't much of a fighter and it didn't take them long to overwhelm me, with two pinning, two punching and one attempting to chew off my fingernails with jagged, unkempt teeth. I know that there were onlookers and people passing by; nobody stopped to help me or to even offer a modicum of moral support. I became bloodied, woozy and eventually relieved of my fingernails from the assault. Then the toughs began loading some of the supplies that I had been collecting for the homeless into their car and into the car of a buddy of theirs who had evidently stopped by during the brawl. As they all got back into the car, the kids began singing the theme to "Rocky" with words they made up on the spot.

> We like to beat the psoriasis dude,
> We LOVE to beat the psoriasis dude,
> We want to beat him from here to there
> Today.
> Beat him now,
> Beat him then,
> Beat his head,
> Do a bend.

And there was much more but the words began to get slurred by something they were licking that must have swollen or numbed their tongues. I always loved the movie but their improvised theme song sort of ruined it for me. A clerk from a nearby nut shop called the police and many of the responding officers were same ones that I had dealt with during the bank incident. They gathered information while keeping their distance and never asked me to roll up my sleeves or expose my back. I told them my story, providing car model, license plate and a love note that had dropped from one kid's pocket. I also refused medical treatment, certain that the paramedics would be adversely affected by my affliction. I called the director of the charity and explained what had occurred in vivid detail. He told me that I was wrong to attempt to function normally with psoriasis and that I would not be welcomed back the following year. And I totally understood – I really did.

A miracle occurred one evening during a boring Presidential debate – miracle is a strong word but there is no other way to term it. In the blink of an eye, all evidence of psoriasis disappeared from my body – gone! My arm, back and nails became clear and even smooth and silky. I'm sure there is a medical explanation but to this day, I have not heard one that holds any water. All I know is that I was cured in a singular moment and the albatross of psoriasis has never returned to dog me again.

Life after psoriasis has been a revelation for me. Food tastes better, social interaction feels "social" and, strangely, my electricity bills have dropped dramatically. My relations with the opposite sex have been much improved and my relations with bank tellers and cops have been essentially without incident, excepting an occasional snide remark or skintight grimace. I can comfortably wear short sleeves without any fear of ridicule or condemnation and if I pull up my shirt to point out a scar or mole, I can do so without psoriasis rearing its ugly head.

A couple of years after the disappearance of the psoriasis, I found myself in a sanitary doctor's office while fighting a dark battle with an uncertain pneumonia. The doctor sported a puzzled look on his ruddy face while conducting his examination and I asked him what the hell was the matter.

"Do you know what psoriasis is?" he asked gravely.

"Um, no", I lied.

"It's a terribly uncomfortable and embarrassing skin disease that pretty much controls the lives of those afflicted. Outside of melanoma, it's probably the worst thing that can happen to your skin."

"Okay. So why are you telling me this?"

"Well," the doctor stammered, "there appears to be a better than fifty-fifty chance that you are developing a hacked-off version of the disease. There seem to be signs of an impending outbreak, or at least possibly so."

"Nope," I said. "Not happening. You're wrong and I will no longer listen to your ass or really anything you have to say."

With that, I stormed out of the quack's office, drove to the nearest available strip club and proceeded to drink myself into a silly, hazardous stupor. When I woke up the following morning in the backseat of my car, I immediately checked for any sign of psoriasis and then raised one eyebrow to indicate a sense of non-maintained trepidation. Yep, that's exactly what I did.

#27

Waitresses That Drink Catsup From a Bottle For a Tip

A GANG-BANGER THAT I had somehow befriended told me that the best places on earth to find waitresses that would drink catsup directly from the bottle for a tip were Auckland, New Zealand and Lone Oak, Texas. I have no idea how he knew this and I also have no idea why I felt driven to verify the claim – I just did. Determining the best places to find waitresses that would drink catsup from a bottle became my number one priority for nearly half a year and during that time, I imagine that I asked around six hundred waitresses to drink catsup from a bottle for a tip. Most simply laughed it off, though a few became upset and several became irate to the point of physical aggression.

But in Lone Oak, nearly every single waitress was agreeable. My first Lone Oak stop was a little diner called "The Smoking Gun", a musty place with wildlife mounted on the walls and creaky hardwood floors that smelled something like spinach. After being seated in an oversized booth, I was greeted by a fifty-something waitress named Muriel, a white grandma-looking lady with a gold tooth and a fake pearl nose ring. She had a raspy smoker's voice that penetrated my soul and kind of seemed to fertilize my virility. In a word, I guess I would describe Muriel as "moldy".

"What can I get you, baby?"

"Someone told me that the chicken-fried steak is good here."

"Oh no, baby. I wouldn't trust the chicken-fried steak."

"OK...so what do you recommend?"

"The best things here are the mollusks. They are grilled *just* right and come with your choice of dipping sauces – chocolate, caramel or strawberry."

"All right," I said. "Bring me an order of mollusks with the chocolate dipping sauce. Also, would you consider drinking catsup direct from a bottle?"

"Sure, sweetie. For a tip I will."

I pulled a five-dollar bill from my wallet and slapped it down onto the table. Muriel smiled, grabbed up the bill and leaned over the table to grab the nearly full bottle of Heinz catsup.

"Bottoms up!" she exclaimed and turned the bottle upside down and put the opening into her mouth. It took a few seconds but the catsup began flowing gradually and I could clearly see the undulations in her throat as it slid it down her throat and into her belly. It was an unbelievable sight and definitely worth the five dollars I had spent. Muriel really seemed to enjoy it and I guess she swallowed half the bottle of catsup before setting it down and wiping off her mouth.

"Thanks, baby! I'll get your mollusks right out to you." She *did* get my mollusks right out to me and she was correct about the quality – they were *good*!

Just down the street from "The Smoking Gun" was another restaurant called "Two Guys and a Burro". This seemed like a kind of local hangout with lots of elderly gentlemen sitting around drinking coffee and smoking cigars. There were framed and autographed photos of celebrities on the wall – Chuck Howley, Willie Nelson, Vin Scully, Pam Tillis, Mark Aguirre, Leonard Nimoy – and I guessed that they must have been visitors to this establishment at some point. "Two Guys and a Burro" had overly bright tiled floors and utilized old barrels and crates in the place of tables and chairs, which I thought added a significant amount of charm.

I found a barrel to sit on and unintentionally began listening to the old men at the next table. One old man was going on and on about the writer Robert Frost. It seems he had once entered a public restroom as Frost was exiting and had been disgusted by the condition Frost had left it in.

"That guy Frost must have had some horrible gastrointestinal diseases and his diet must've been pretty fucked up, too. That was the smell of death…it really was. And he left that toilet clogged as hell with his mess and I can tell you right now it was a sight I'll never forget. Never! But he was a good writer, I guess."

"You could say that he 'frosted' that goddamn bathroom," another old guy chimed in, cackling to high heaven.

"Can I help you?" The teenaged waitress stood before me – pad and pencil in hand -- and I was immediately impressed with her professionalism and level of cuteness.

"How's the chicken-fried steak?"

"Best in Lone Oak!" she bubbled. "Want some? I can bring it to you."

"OK," I replied. "I'll have the chicken-fried steak and a pudding pop, if you have any."

"I think we do."

"I was also wondering if you would be willing to drink some catsup direct from the bottle."

"Absolutely!" she bubbled. "I'll do it for a tip!"

I pulled another five-dollar bill from my wallet and handed it to the teenager. She stuffed it into her apron pocket and told me that she would be right back. She returned in mere seconds with a bottle of somewhat watery Heinz that was a little bit less than half full. Wordlessly, she tipped the open bottle into her mouth and began heartily sucking the catsup greedily into her mouth. Like Muriel, she really got into it and it really seemed to me that she loved performing this task. Later, she brought out my meal but, since I was still full from the mollusks from down the street, I gave my plate of food to the old men at the next table. They thanked me profusely and dug right in, attacking like a pack of hungry wolves in more ways than just one.

I checked out two more diners in Lone Oak – I think the only other two in town – and at both places, the waitresses drank catsup from a bottle for a five-dollar tip. One was a Dairy Queen and the lady that took my order happily swallowed the catsup for the tip and on the condition that I played an Eddie Rabbit song on the jukebox. The other restaurant was called "The Pretty Skillet" and since I was the only customer there, two different waitresses were vying for my attention and both of them took turns drinking catsup from the same bottle. I was glad to give them both a five-dollar tip and sat back and enjoyed the show.

Lone Oak was certainly a gold mine for waitresses that would drink catsup from a bottle for a tip. I decided to check out some other East Texas towns – Campbell, Lindale, Big Sandy, Van, Gilmer – and had no luck at all in finding a waitress that would drink catsup from a bottle for a tip. In fact, I think I was nearly arrested because several waitresses felt uncomfortable and even scared by my request. In Troup, I got my ass kicked by a jealous boyfriend who thought I was propositioning his waitress girlfriend with some kind of big city slang for oral. I held my own for a while but he was much younger and stronger than me and it really wasn't much of a fight in the end.

Yes, the gang-banger was certainly right about Lone Oak – but he had also mentioned Auckland, New Zealand and I wondered just how right he was about that. Knowing in my heart that there was only one way to find out for certain, I began saving for the extremely expensive airfare to and from Auckland. Even purchasing my ticket sixty days out, I was looking at an expenditure of nearly three thousand dollars for just the airfare – and I would still need a place to stay and stuff to eat and whatnot. I trimmed abruptly from my daily living expenses and short-paid a couple of credit cards and was able to save the funds necessary to make the trip.

The flight was an arduous, never-ending affair and when I arrived in Auckland, I was probably a bit spacey, as well as a little nutty. I had arranged to stay with a Polynesian couple with unpronounceable first names – they told me to call them Spike and Mary. Spike met me at the airport and by that point I had totally forgotten why I had come to Auckland; when Spike asked, I told him that I was there to hang shelving. In the car on the ride to their house, I remembered my mission and laid out my endeavor for Spike. He seemed somewhat puzzled but nodded along indulgently.

After a drive of about an hour, we arrived at their home. It was rather small but toasty and obviously livable with just the right amount of creature comforts. Spike and Mary were in their early fifties and turned out to be very congenial hosts, taking me to a Netball match and to the Aotea Square to hunt crafts and canned goods. They had decent command of the English language but often took to conversing in their native tongue, especially when I was sauced or had to blow my nose. I liked them a lot and they seemed to like me, allowing me to borrow their only car when I decided the time had come to explore on my own.

And the time had definitely come for me to explore on my own; I was there to find waitresses that would drink catsup from the bottle for a tip and I needed to proceed with my mission. The first place I tried was an odd little place queerly called "The Mousetrap". I thought it was a terrible name for a diner but the aroma that drifted outside into the street was intoxicating. I went inside and found a place to sit amid what seemed like a huge group of disorderly drunks, who were cussing up a storm and calling each other "philly" and "rhino". A little old lady fought her way through the raucous bunch and came to wait on me.

"What smells so good?" I asked.

"Oh, that's the grease-fried sodium. We're the only place in the city that makes it. It's very fattening but also really, really addictive. Would you like a plate?"

"Um, no…I'm not a big fan of sodium. What I would really like is if you would consider drinking catsup direct from the bottle. Do you think you could?"

"On your way, creep. We don't serve your kind here."

She turned and started animatedly describing my request to the rowdy crew and I made the instinctive decision to get immediately out of that place. Just down the road, I ducked into another little eatery called "Chandler's". It appeared nice enough and was populated with what seemed like a friendly crowd; I could easily discern that all of them were eating barbeque brisket and olive loaf sandwiches while washing it all down with pints of Fosters or at least the equivalent. It was a little dark and I tentatively made my way through the dining room and located a place to sit. It only took a few seconds for the waitress to come over.

"Hello! Welcome to Chandler's! Can I start you out with an appetizer or beverage?" Her nametag said "Rhoda" and this was a beautiful lady, probably in her mid-twenties with long blonde hair and a picturesque figure that left little the imagination. She made the waitress garb look great, though she was wearing flip flops which I thought was a bit strange in a restaurant. But my brain took to Rhoda immediately and I wondered how long she would be a part of my life.

"Well, I don't have a menu so…"

"We don't have menus here," she interrupted. "Our appetizers are olive loaf sandwiches and sand scallops. Our beverages are Fosters and Fresca. And for the main course, we serve barbeque brisket."

"None of that sounds too good to me," I stammered. "Do you have catsup?"

"Absolutely! Did you want to make a meal out of catsup?"

"Actually, I was hoping you would. You see, I was told that Auckland…"

Again Rhoda cut me off. "So you're one of those guys that want to see waitresses drink catsup from the bottle." She sounded stern but not at all unfriendly. "Listen, that's a myth. Waitresses don't do that here. I've heard that Auckland has this reputation for some reason but I can assure you that none of us do it. I don't think *any* waitresses anywhere do it."

"Oh, they do," I corrected her. "There's this place called Lone Oak, Texas where every waitress in town will do it for a tip – I'm not kidding."

"Lone Oak, Texas," she murmured. "I think I've heard of that. Sounds like a magical place. How much of a tip do they get?"

"Five American dollars is standard. I don't know how negotiable it is but I can tell you firsthand that five dollars definitely gets the deed done."

"Wow…I guess those waitresses in Lone Oak, Texas can make quite a bit of extra money, eh?"

"I think they do," I concurred.

"Maybe I'm waiting tables in the wrong bloody place!" Rhoda said and started to laugh loud enough to warrant a hearty "ssshhh" from the leather-jacketed butch cashier. Rhoda lowered her voice. "Look, I would do it for you but I would be setting a bad precedent, or at least I fear I would. First, I'm drinking catsup from a bottle for a tip and next thing you know, I'm stripping my clothes off for a tip. I just think its bad form, really. I hope you understand."

"Sure I do – no hard feelings. You're actually saving me a bunch of time because now I don't have to bother with going a bunch of other places and trying to get their waitresses to do it. You've saved me time and trouble. I wish you the best."

Rhoda just smiled sweetly as I got up from the table and headed out the door. Auckland, New Zealand had been a *major* disappointment and my gang-banger friend could not have been more wrong. I had wasted thousands of dollars and much valuable time chasing something that simply did not exist. True, I had met a few colorful characters but I could not justify the expense involved in meeting these colorful characters.

Further, I had wasted five days of my life and these days could not be retrieved or relived – they were gone forever.

I found myself making the short drive out to Lone Oak every so often for the next few years. I was comforted by the willingness of these waitresses to drink catsup from the bottle for a tip and I was fortified by their brazen rejection of all incarnations of conventionality. I'm not really sure why I eventually quit going out there; just fell out of the habit, I guess. But I can never eat a catsup-based meatloaf without reflecting on the bravery of these strong-willed ladies and it's sad to me that some of them will probably die sooner rather than later.

#28

● ● ● ● ● ● ● ● ● ● ● ● ● ● ● ● ● ● ● ●

Alien Encounters and a Guy in a Coma

UNLIKE MOST PEOPLE, I have had only one alien encounter and though it was illustrious, it was really nothing to write home about. I know folks that have experienced dozens and dozens of alien encounters, many of which involved actual spaceships, space travel and such. Almost everyone I know has gone through no fewer than sixteen such encounters and for a long time I wondered if a real alien encounter was in the cards for me. I also began to possess creeping doubts about the validity of many of the stories that I heard and wondered if the entire world might be pulling a cruel prank on the likes of me.

Everything changed on my 41st birthday when I experienced my one and only alien encounter. The day began in fairly ordinary fashion, with me firing up a crock-pot full of outdated raisins and jarring the sweet and sour liquid they produced for future usage at a party or maybe in some kind of pageant. I had set my brand new VCR to record a documentary about the life and times of Lon Hinkle and was dismayed to find that the tape had somehow been obscenely melted inside of the malfunctioning device. I was hunched over my VCR using a tablespoon to clean out the melted and twisted tape when I noticed something that seemed like really bad breath wafting in from behind. I turned around to see Jack Nicklaus wearing a hideous green jacket and making hokey baboon faces. Before I could say a word, Jack Nicklaus transformed into Gertrude Stein, who then turned into a semi-naked female paralegal with a notepad and a pencil.

"What the hell is this?" I screamed out to no one in particular. The semi-naked paralegal recoiled just a tad and then became Morris Day. Morris Day began singing a song about Wesley Snipes and the power of the pen while snorting an over-filled stein of miniature yams. Morris Day then transformed into the mailman from Cheers, who quickly turned into a black Gary Cooper with a broken tennis racket and a blank piece of notebook paper stuck to his forehead.

This was a truly weird happening for me and I found myself perspiring profusely from the mouth and ears. It didn't take long for me to realize that I was experiencing full scale alien contact and also that it wasn't too terribly dangerous; in fact, there seemed to be no jeopardy whatsoever. I watched intently as the black Gary Cooper skipped feverishly around my well-lighted living room (evidently with a song or something similar in his heart) and soon settled onto the plush couch. Almost the very second he sat his ass down, the black Gary Cooper became the female Ray Davies and began humming "Lola" in a sheer and courageous falsetto. When the song was complete, the female Ray Davies used offset eyes to set fire to every bit of my remaining winter wear, which left me with no further winter wear to speak of. Of course, this sucked but at least I lived in Texas where winters tended to be mild and whatnot.

"OK, so what's next?" I looked straight at the female Ray Davies and inadvertently phrased the question as a quasi macho challenge. The female Ray Davies smirked like a banshee and then turned into an overly tall Rolando Blackman for a couple of seconds and then into Myrna Loy carrying a transparent suitcase.

I knew that I would never forgive myself if I didn't earnestly attempt to make some kind of tangible contact with this creature. Myrna Loy was so pale as to almost be invisible but I did see obvious signs of a mouth, eyes, ears and various and assorted lymph nodes.

"Hello. I am a tried and true earthling. Where are you from?" I asked earnestly. Myrna Loy just stared at me, blinking with full and comforting regularity.

"Are you here for some reason? Can I help you in some way? Would you like a drink?"

Myrna Loy said nothing but just then her slender hips began gyrating violently and multi-colored sprays began shooting from six different locations on her body. The sprays shot gracefully through the air and landed onto my carpet but disappeared on contact – no stains, no mess, no nothing. Without warning, she transformed into Daniel Defoe with a bloody pig's foot hung casually around his neck and he appeared indignant at the scene *I* was apparently causing.

"Hey, I loved 'Everybody's Business is Nobody's Business'. You really stuck it to 'em. I thought your work was very articulate, very nice." Daniel Defoe just stared at me as I spoke and sort of hovered up and down a little – kind of like a ghost would but he did not appear at all "ghost-like". The ghastly pig's foot was dripping blood but again nothing appeared on my carpet. It was surreal but also quite clean.

"Can you speak? Do you know English?" I was becoming increasingly frustrated by the lack of verbal contact, other than the female Ray Davies' humming. If this was indeed an alien (as I suspected it was), I would assume that they would have researched our culture and arrived prepared to engage in some type of meaningful interaction which, in my opinion, would have to involve verbal contact and even a bit of sparring, if necessary. But this alien seemed to have nothing meaningful to say, which I had no choice but to interpret as aloofness.

The alien switched from Daniel Defoe to a tanned and healthy Bert Convey holding a large microphone from some sort of seventies game show. Bert Convey was smiling and his eyes were dancing like a lithe Florence Nightingale – he truly seemed happy to be in my living room. And then, to my great relief, he spoke utilizing discernible English.

"Consider yourself counted." With that, Bert Convey disappeared like an amputated toe, leaving behind only the microphone, a pack of spearmint gum and a repaired version of the Lon Hinkle tape. First things being first, I sat down and watched the tape, which I found slow in parts but nonetheless enlightening and at times even endearing. Then I phoned my friend Wes, who had been involved in something like 86 different alien interactions and spoke of writing a book one day.

"I finally met an alien!" I told him, and went on for about an hour or more describing the incident in elevated detail and also offering personal commentary concerning the overall deed and presentation.

"Yeah," he said, "I had one like that. There weren't as many personnel changes but I remember it appearing as Ron Svoboda, Randal "Tex" Cobb and I believe Zelda Fitzgerald -- and maybe Jane Wyman, I'm not totally sure. It kept watching me and doing tricks and stuff but didn't seem interested in talking until the very end after a couple of hours. It told me 'mind your children' and, of course, I have no children. I have never understood the message."

"They're not doing this for nothing," I said. "They must have a reason. Don't you think it's important for us to figure out what they want?"

But Wes just waved his hand as if swatting a buzzing fly. "Don't worry about it. It's nothing. Don't waste your time overanalyzing these things." He trailed off dismissively and sort of drifted away – I didn't hear a dial tone but it was obvious that he was no longer part of the conversation and it was time for me to get out.

It was more than a little shocking to me that I got pretty much the same reaction from everyone I told – both of my brothers, my mother, a group of friends from my soccer called "Gimpy", Orlando Cepeda, my body doctor, Gordon Keith. The consensus was that it was no big deal and I shouldn't worry too much about it. Some of them even laughed at me because it was such a "minor league" experience. Do I wish that my alien experience had included getting physically probed or being taken away in some kind of cool spacecraft? Of course I do. But that did not happen for me and I think it's important that I appreciate the encounter that I *did have* and not preoccupy myself with the superior experiences of others. I'm just glad that my day finally came – I really am.

Several years have passed and I have never again been visited by any kind of alien being. I don't believe that there is an age limit on this type of encounter so I definitely remain hopeful. But if it doesn't happen again for me, that's OK too. There are a myriad of other things that I desire to see and experience in my life – professional sap extraction, Christian fortification, a height/weight proportionate Hispanic lounge singer, a jovial rendition of the Hindenburg event and maybe a dead moose or two if I get lucky. Thus, life goes on and I must endeavor to keep moving forward.

Unquestionably, my alien interaction had a profound impact on the way I lead my life and the manner in which I handle crisis situations and whatnot. But there has also been a troubling side effect: Since that day, I find that I can no longer eat any food that's not completely – and I mean *completely* -- soaked in milk (which can be especially embarrassing in a fine dining environment). Oh, and I'm also irresistibly attracted to anything with velvet and transgender snake charmers with those dangly pocket watches.

#29

Untimely Demise in the Malacca Strait

DURING MY FINAL VOYAGE through the Malacca Strait, I inexplicably lost hearing in one ear and casually befriended a jocular native who turned out to be a descendent of Count Giacomo Leopardi. His name was evidently Duke and he contended that he was some kind of leprechaun, though I was somewhat dubious. The leprechauns that I have read about in literature always seemed to be dainty, mischievous little sprites bent on wreaking forms of havoc sequentially from left to right and occasionally flat onto prone, flexible bodies. Duke was not at all mischievous and seemed a little bit addicted to artificial flavoring – unlike any leprechaun known to man.

Duke taught me how to tie what he called a "prophecy knot" which, from what I understand, is a twisted, double-stacked knot in any beige or white rope used to rescue a solicitor or his family. He also counseled me about methods to combat my receding hairline and the trouble I encountered with superficial consternation. Duke was an attentive, altruistic comrade who swore an affection for rock-climbing and wore his ball cap backwards before it was exactly hip. He enjoyed jelly and nearly any brand name syrup or mustard, as long as the container had a squeeze top, which he assumed made everything smoother.

I was deeply saddened when Duke passed away from a bout of Rocky Mountain Spotted Fever acquired somewhere along the way. When he sensed that the end was near, he called me in close and groaned that he coveted a burial at sea. I assured him in my most reliable voice that I would respect his wishes but I never felt right about it. After he passed, I agonized for hours and hours, finally resolving that I just couldn't go through with it. I feared his body being ripped to shreds by sharks or something even worse.

Nearing the west end of the Strait, I spotted a tiny village made from straw and beets and concluded that I should turn Duke's body in. I anchored the boat in the shallows, tossed the body over my shoulder and headed for the dusty, dry sand. The villagers spotted me on my way in and nearly three dozen of them stood by naked as I struggled through waist high water to shore. The village elders stepped forward and I explained the situation, using only my hands and expressive eyes since they spoke no English. The village elders accepted the body greedily – too greedily – which left me with a goddamn funny feeling. No funny "haha", but funny "strange".

#30

A Pretty Wife and Orange Drumsticks

As a lifelong lover of rock music, it is the great disappointment in my life that I was not blessed with one speck of musical talent – nada. I cannot sing, I cannot play an instrument, I cannot dance and I really seem to have no musical inclinations whatsoever. Despite this, I have always idolized these musicians of whom I am so envious; I've purchased their recordings, I've attended their concerts and I've sung and played along whenever I've heard their music on the radio or perhaps in a patio setting. I would spend fortunes I do not have to spend time in the shoes of Eddie Vedder, Dave Groel, Eric Clapton, Burton Cummings, Todd Rundgren and their therapists. So, as you can well imagine, I jumped hard at the opportunity when a small circle of friends formed a band and asked me to come along and bang the drum.

I had never drummed in my life but my buddies assured me that would not pose any kind of significant problem. They planned to compose music heavy on verbal symmetry that would require nothing more than a very simple, repetitive drumbeat in conjunction with a thumping bass guitar. The guys thought that my personality would mesh well with the rest of the band and all they wanted from me was to purchase a drum kit and to throw in a few meaningless or meaningful lyrics here, there and about. Of course, I was agreeable and some; thus, a 1:00am deep night summit was scheduled at a local IHOP for us to meet and discuss, among other things, musical theory, philosophical ideals and a small but growing conflict at the Algerian border. After about two hours and some seriously high stacks of syrup-laden pancakes, the rock group "Followers Menu" was born.

The name was the brainchild of the anointed lead guitarist, a mercurial yet normally affable chap aptly named Richard. Richard explained to us that the phrase "Followers Menu" was a big player in black magic circles and in the zany literature of the occult. None of the rest of us had ever heard the phrase but Richard painstakingly sketched out a pie chart that indicated how popular the band would become with that name...and how drearily unpopular we would be without it. It was a truly powerful presentation and it seemed inane at that point to seriously consider any of the other names that had been put forth (Pillow Talk, The Creatures, Damien's Doorstep, Silly Petrified Dung, and The Wayward Laces with Larry and Frank).

The first real rehearsal took place the very next evening in the garage of our lead singer Douglas. Douglas was around thirty at the time with a slightly overweight yet very pretty wife and a little baby of probably six or seven months. He worked part-time as an inventory specialist and he and his wife were renting this squared house on Moon Drive for something like $500 per month (according to Richard), which seemed like a pretty good deal to me. The other members were the bass player Kenny, a very quiet, pale dude who only spoke when spoken to and the rhythm guitarist Monti, a public relations dream who dressed immaculately, quoted the Bible and sought to make friends with nearly everyone he met. He was also a talented and versatile musician, extremely skilled on the piano and harpsichord as well as several forms of guitar.

That initial rehearsal was essentially uneventful. I had not yet purchased my drum kit so I pretty much sat around guzzling mint juleps while the three of them jammed, physically praised one another and toyed with riffs and lyrics. My overall impression was that this could be a very good band indeed and I became just a bit anxious about my lack of experience on the drums. I guess I didn't convey this concern at the time because they were kindly inclusive, soliciting my opinion on the music and asking for count-ins at various points in the proceedings.

The following day, I went to a local hip music store – the brick and mortar kind -- and purchased the least expensive new set they had. There were two snares, a bass and a cymbal along with a couple of handy foot pedals and it seemed pretty damn complicated to me, but I consoled myself with the idea that I would never be using most of the stuff anyway. Because I wasn't too worried about practicing since the band planned on keeping the drum parts simple, I arranged to have the set delivered directly to Douglas' garage on Moon Drive, where it was signed for by his pretty wife Ginger, probably while holding the baby in one arm or the other.

We did not practice that day because Kenny had to go to court for some traffic tickets but we did get together again the next day for a lively session. Richard had already written a complete song and demoed it for us, plaintively singing the words while playing a tasteful lead guitar. He gave his written lyrics to Douglas and got together with Kenny, Monti and me individually to examine our parts in the song. The song was called "Da Pope Got Da Flu" and my part was literally nothing more than using my pedal to hit the bass in a solemn, unchanging rhythm -- I did not even get the chance to use my hot new florescent orange drumsticks! The song was about a friendly and unassuming Pope who contracted the flu and was forced to cancel some appearances, supermarket openings and even a chunk of assorted whatnot. It was not a particularly meaningful song but it was tuneful and tidy, winding up in a mere two and half minutes, and Douglas sang it expressively and with emphatically crinkled eyebrows.

Even though my part in the song was next to nothing, I was really feeling like part of the band, part of something potentially special. After playing through "Da Pope Got Da Flu" several times, the group jammed a bit on snippets of old standards and even some experimental improvisation. I got the opportunity to use my florescent orange drumsticks on the surprised snares and I was digging the way it sounded. I pounded the beat just as I had been drumming my fingers on the steering wheel to the Stones and The Who for years. I even made my mark during the jam, improvising a rat a tat tat...rat tat a tat...rat tat that made the other guys stop what they were doing and stare in quiet approval.

The initial stated goal of the band was to create enough of a mixture of new songs and cover arrangements to begin doing public gigs and maybe even a few county fairs. This was thrilling to me and I threw everything I had into our rehearsals and was even given the opportunity to contribute to the composition of some of the new songs. One such song was entitled, "God's Day Off", into which I contributed the line, "I'd pluck my own eye to see the rise, and try not to laugh when everyone dies". Another new song was called "Simmer Down With That Mohawk" and I wrote the following verse:

I flitter about with the greatest of ease
While diverting my gaze when an old lady pees.
I'll fuck up a dude who responds to my show
And foster the scene with preeminent glow
(While stiffening like dead Edgar Allen Poe).

When we were eventually hired for our first gig, we were all really stoked at the idea of performing live. The club that hired us was called Russell's Beehive and was located on the very edge of the southern end of the Dallas entertainment district, just a bit off of Lamar Street near Interstate 30. The club was cozy, accommodating a crowd of just below eighty, and was pretty well known locally for its potent martinis and desperately sassy restroom attendants. The five of us arrived together that evening in a rented cargo van, with my drum set consuming most of the available space. When we walked in, Richard immediately began talking business and sports with the cigar-chewing owner while the rest of us started assembling and setting up our equipment on the four-foot high makeshift stage. It's hard to express how exciting it was to be at this real club as a real, working band preparing to ply our trade for an interested audience – it was insane, really.

At or around 9:00 pm, I struck the snare as Kenny clawed the strings of his moaning bass and Followers Menu was off the first tee! Monti and Richard commenced their wild strumming and Douglas launched into the first searing words of "Da Pope Got Da Flu": "I couldn't help but giggle like a dick when da Pope fainted from effects of da flu…" The audience seemed to love us and it was certainly an evening none of us would forget. By the time we closed two hours later with a loveably ragged rendition of "Twist and Shout", we were exhilarated, sweaty and sorely in need of a shave or worse. We sat at the bar for another two hours that night drinking the free beers and cocktails sent to us from appreciative members of the lingering crowd, feeling every bit like true and splendid rock stars – glamorous to the hilt.

We gathered at Douglas' house the following day, dining on spicy meat pies prepared by the pretty Ginger. The five of us sat around the pronged and comfortable kitchen table chewing on the meat pies and reflecting on our exploits of the previous night. Monti loved everything about it, thought it was absolutely and unconditionally perfect. Douglas was pleased except for the fact that four members of the audience kept singing out of key and loudly along to the cover songs, which evidently distracted him or something worse. Kenny said it was too damn hot. I told everyone that I thought it was a mesmerizing and thought-provoking experience to be up on stage playing the role of rock gods.

Richard simply sat listening to us, looking stern and saying nothing for a long, long while. Something was obviously weighing heavily on his mind and he began to look as if he might burst or something equally as horrific as bursting. He then reached into his silver trimmed guitar case and pulled out the folded entertainment section of The Dallas Morning News; it seems that someone from the paper had reviewed our show and Richard was obviously distressed.

"The fucking Dallas Morning News torched us. They called us amateurs and called our songs sophomoric." Richard hesitated, and then continued with carefully measured words. "They called our drummer the worst in the history of rock and roll…the absolute worst – and they put it in goddamned capital italics!"

We sat around the table in a sorry silence for quite a while – maybe fifteen minutes or more – just looking at walls and into space, avoiding each other's eyes. The ever-congenial Monti finally stood up to speak.

"Guys, we started this band to have a good time – nothing more. Who gives a fuck what the paper or anyone else says about us. We had fun last night, didn't we? We all murmured in tacit agreement. "Right! I know I did. So let's not worry about what people think and have a *blast* doing this thing. This is *a blast*! We get to play goddamn rock stars! This is the coolest thing I've ever done – I know that for sure."

No doubt Monti was right and his pep talk definitely lifted our spirits. We played a gig the following weekend, skipped a week and then played every weekend for the next three months or so. The band was getting tighter -- both on-stage and off -- and the crowds really began responding positively to the new songs, actually preferring them to the cover versions we performed. Followers Menu gained a following of a few dozen fans that began joining us all over town at whatever venue we played. We got to know them each individually, especially their leader and organizer Mindy, a youthful English professor at the University of Texas at Arlington. She started a fan club, advertised our band all over the UTA campus and began an indiscreet sexual relationship with the suddenly balding Douglas.

The unmistakable fact is that the other guys in the band also began affairs with many of the girls and ladies that attended our shows. I guess there is just something about skinny, pasty white, drunken musicians that drives the women wild. It was all too weird for me and I actually abstained when it came to hooking up with any of our "groupies". I usually just played the shows, hung out for a couple of beers at the bar and then l left as the steamy making-out and groping sessions began between our band and their chosen playmates.

We kept on rehearsing and composing new material on a nearly daily basis. I wrote all of the lyrics on a risqué little ditty called "Play-Do in the Hole" that Richard turned into a full-fledged rock anthem by the time he was finished with it. In what seemed like no time, we had something like thirty original compositions and we thought they all sounded terrific. In fact, the consensus was that the time had come to record our debut album.

Richard seemed to know tons of people and soon he had lined up an employed producer that was willing to work with us. This producer had attended two of our shows and liked what he heard in the original stuff and was intrigued by the sheer animal magnetism the band displayed, anxious to capture the energy on tape. However, the producer was adamant about one concession that the band must make: Followers Menu *had* to find another drummer – either a professional drummer or a raw and talented drummer that could be groomed. The current drummer (yours truly) would simply not suffice…not in any way, shape or form.

The band sat me down at Douglas' one early afternoon and laid everything out on the pronged kitchen table. I could tell that they felt terrible about the way this was working out for me but I also knew that they had begun to aspire for greatness and that I was nothing but an irritating obstacle. They had already found another drummer; his street name was Chico and he was supposedly a second or third cousin of Sheila E. and an avid outdoorsman with size fifteen feet. I told them that I understood and that there were no hard feelings at all. And there really weren't at that time. They had taken me on a helluva whirlwind five-month ride of a lifetime and no one could take that away from me. We stood up and shook hands all around, fighting back what would have been extremely feminine tears. I went into the living room to say goodbye to the pretty Ginger and the baby. Ginger stood up and we shared a lingering, breathless hug; I whispered into her ear that I had always wanted to "screw her" and she whispered back that we could do it but no more than seven times – that was her rule. I asked her if she meant seven different occasions or only seven thrusts on one occasion. She replied that her rule was seven different occasions with no limit on the amount of thrusts and I told her that was good because seven thrusts would only last a few seconds and that was not enough time.

I avoided the temptation to attend any of the Followers Menu shows but I did keep up with their exploits through the papers and through word of mouth. The group really hit their stride and began playing a number of high profile gigs, opening for Duran Duran, The Bangles and The GoGos (and, according to rumor, hooking up with some of the GoGos physically that night after the concert). Before long, Followers Menu had become the preeminent local band and began to develop a cult following across the state and even across southern areas of the country. Since they had kept my drum set and continued to use songs to which I had contributed, I could not help but feel like at least a small part of everything that was going on. However, when I ran into the group at a Williams Chicken in Garland and walked over to say hello, they absolutely ignored me – pretended I didn't exist at all. I knew then that none of my contributions – however big or small – were the least bit appreciated by my former friends. It was a rude awakening for me but certainly a lesson learned.

Followers Menu released seven different and distinctive CD's, each of which was very well received by critics though they didn't sell particularly well. They never charted with any of their songs except for a song they had written that was covered by an eight-man group from Indonesia, whose version peaked at number twelve in the United States charts and shot up to number eight in Great Britain. I really believe that Followers Menu could have been one of the greatest rock bands of our generation but, unfortunately for them, things happened within the band that created a dissention, which ultimately resulted in a stereotypical ugly breakup. I never knew for sure what the problems were but the scuttlebutt around town was that the pretty Ginger had been carrying on long-term affairs with Richard AND Kenny and that Douglas had found out in a note from the baby.

The newspaper reported that during what ended up being Followers Menu's final concert, a violent fistfight broke out on stage between Richard and Douglas. Douglas got the better of things, bloodying Richard's nose and mouth with a barrage of massive punches to the face. A demented Richard managed to pull out a chunk of Douglas' thinning hair and left a bite imprint on Douglas' right bicep. The owner of the club banned Followers Menu for life and their formerly impressive group of supporters pretty much abandoned them after this sad and sorry display.

Followers Menu certainly earned its place in history as one of music's most enigmatic outfits. I think that the life of this band can be best described in a passage from one of the songs on their album "Followers Menu IV: Don't be Hatin' Da Menu".

Sometimes when your drummer sucks
You have to sack him like a bag of whack.
And often when your tongue is tired
It's time to be lunching on a crazy, hatin' bagel.

Was it conceivable that the other fellows in Followers Menu were nothing more than petulant carpetbaggers? Yes, in retrospect there doesn't appear to be much question about it. And that is just fine with me – it really the hell is.

#32

A Detailed Plan to Save EVERYONE

IT WASN'T TOO FAR back that I became determined to create and enact a detailed plan to save the world in which we live. There are many – especially the fortunate – who would argue that the world does not need saving or that it's not mine to save in the first place. To those people, I would form my mouth in such a way as to deliver an energized "bullshit!" in response; to me, it's evident that our troubled world *does* need saving and I have no reservations about claiming it as mine to save... none whatsoever. Crime and disease run rampant, our environment is polluted with man made toxins, priests are fondling boys and Jerry Jones has turned the Dallas Cowboys into some kind of damn laughingstock. The world is in need of an overhaul and I had decided that I might be just the man for the job.

I don't subscribe to the utopian point of view that we need to eliminate war, religion, possessions, et al to accomplish a peaceful, harmonious existence for mankind. In my opinion, that wouldn't work; I believe we need *some* war, *some* religion and tons of possessions to reach the stated goal. What we *don't* need are warmongers, violent religious zealots or poorly maintained sewer systems. I think the sewer system thing is crucial because sweet smells and aromas go hand-in-hand with tranquility and enriched fulfillment. People are at their absolute worst when confronted with foul stenches such as those in dirty bathrooms, slaughterhouses or areas with rancid, standing water. Think about it:

Have you ever had a pleasant conversation with someone in a restroom that had been recently fouled by another who was sick, overfed and possibly overweight? Of course not, it's impossible and you know it.

Also, violence would obviously need to be curbed by, according to my calculations, 82%. To accomplish this, we would need to enlist the aid of the worlds top thirteen impressionists, three dozen speed readers, Nancy Grace and Sammy Sosa. With the impressionists and the speed-readers paving the way, the team of Grace and Sosa (nicknamed "Grosa") would be free to utilize their philosophical charm along with their clinical yet robust dance moves to entrance violent offenders into relative inaction for reasonably long periods of time. In effect, Grosa would impose a "cease fire" of sorts on those desiring to inflict harm with a mind game that would be hopeless for potential perpetrators to combat.

My complete and comprehensive plan contained a dozen steps to a "saved" world and I am pleased to share them with you, provided you don't make fun of me.

- Heavily, *heavily* perfumed bathrooms, sewer systems, slaughterhouses, teenagers, bedrooms, tennis shoes, rivers and streams, landfills, mortuaries, chopping blocks, jails and prisons, driver's license bureaus, foreign-owned convenience stores, hockey gear, thrift stores and the entire city of Texarkana (both the Arkansas and Texas sides).
- Coordinated peace missive by impressionists, speed-readers, Nancy Grace and Sammy Sosa.
- Utilization of current technological advances to invent a tiny, once-daily pill to eliminate the human need of food and other forms of nourishment, squelching the scourge of hunger and saving the lives of many living forms of meat-based products.
- Immediate cancellation of all high-wire acts and circus entertainment, which could, in essence, de-fry the minds of thousands of white-trash pinheads and many of their helpless heirs.
- Taking religion to a new level by instituting a law that requires masks to be worn during any and all in-church activities. Worshippers would be allowed to choose between masks of Jesus, the Devil, Jimmy Carter, Pamela Anderson

and Osip Mandelstam and would not be allowed to change masks for a period of three years after their original designation. Additionally, Dire Straits' "Sultans of Swing" would be required listening at each and every service or communal gathering.

- Establishment of a single worldwide monetary system that would be tied to the value of gold, silver, coal, stamps and baseball cards and could be utilized for the purchase of perfume, toll tags, sporting event tickets and apparatus used to tie up your partner.

- Abolishment of all traditional home owners associations and, in their place, the appointment of a committee of twenty-something year-old douche bags to rule on yard appearance, building codes, sidewalk upkeep, tree and shrubbery overgrowth, fence and gate matters, the Peter Principal and which moms are hot and which are not. These committees would also oversee all issues pertaining to closed-door sexual matters and groceries.

- Consolidation of television options to just sixteen channels worldwide (one children's channel, one porn channel, four network channels, one black entertainment channel, two music channels, one news channel and six true crime channels). Television would only air for eighteen hours per day and in black and white – no colors would be allowable.

- Imprisonment of all of the world's leaders, including the entire United States Senate and 93% of the British Parliament, in a sprawling village of isolated teepees on the outskirts of Boise with no running water, no social media, limited insect repellent and corn cobs in place of pillows on their matching rock-hard bedding sets.

- Conversion of all mathematical equations, pie charts, mileage signage, skin pigment grafts, dental records, hair salon square footage, musical instrumentation, eye glass prescriptions and city maps to the standard metric system in a memorable, week-long marathon conversion process that would be monitored by three skinny minority scientists from somewhere within the state of Alabama.

- Public bathrooms would not only be heavily, *heavily* perfumed but would also cease to be segregated by sex. Men and women would perform their natural (and unnatural) bathroom acts in the same public bathrooms at the same time and the space saved would be utilized for periodic patch destruction and extreme carcass mummification.
- Dilution of the alcoholic content of all of the world's liquors by a full sixty percent with a patented, concentrated purification effort by an army of homegrown chemists with nothing but time on their hands. The alcohol reduction would serve as a steep warning to those in the habit of cracking their damn knuckles in ironic barrel-chested splendor and also those who pee too much.

I truly believe that the implementation of my twelve steps would not only make the world a significantly better place to live, but it might just save the human race from itself. Think about it – if everyone were required to wear some kind of mask during religious worship, the potential for violence would seem to become radically lessened. Imagine that you are mad at a Catholic and your madness has advanced to the point that you might want to physically attack a Catholic, any Catholic. Well, as you approach a Catholic target, you would find yourself standing face to face with Jimmy Carter or even Jesus. And who would want to attack Jimmy Carter or Jesus? It's unthinkable really. By limiting television options to sixteen selected black and white channels, our young people would find themselves practically forced to interact with their peers and their parents and I'm certain that our collective communication skills would improve markedly. Each of the twelve steps would result in a positive outcome that would play a role in our overall long-term happiness and perpetual well-being.

Convincing an influential public official to listen to me and take me seriously was certainly a challenge. I started at the local level and was laughed out of quite a few town hall meetings until a certain Texas State Senator saw something redeeming in my practiced presentation. He didn't like all of the twelve steps but he loved the idea of getting rid of the stink and he also favored men and women sharing the same public bathrooms. In fact, it turns out that he had campaigned on the sharing of bathrooms and though he received some negative press on the subject, he still won his election with ease.

The State Senator took me to Austin to meet the Lieutenant Governor in an office full of empty baggies on the third floor. The Lieutenant Governor shrewdly pointed out that the invention of a "food pill" might take care of the stink and sewage problem all by itself. I agreed that it would have some limited positive impact but pointed out that the human body would always produce waste and that it would invariably smell bad. He loved the idea of a single worldwide monetary system and also spoke excitedly about the prospect of abolishing homeowners associations. He seemed kind of neutral on the idea of imprisoning world leaders outside of Boise but generally thought highly enough of my ideas to walk me fifty yards down to the Governor's palatial office.

This Governor, who reputedly aspired to become a United States President, shook my hand congenially, smiled warmly and offered me a comfortable seat and a cold bottle of Nehi. I admired his shelves full of trophies, plaques and photos of sports and entertainment celebrities. He admired my watch and was taken aback that I had paid only $35 at the Terrell Walmart. When the conversation moved to my twelve steps, his brow became furrowed and the tone of his voice dipped low.

"Listen, you can't imprison world leaders in Boise."

"*Outside* Boise," I corrected him.

"Whatever," he said. "Problem is that the citizens would have no direction, no leadership. Lawlessness would run rampant in the damn streets."

"No sir, I think you're dead wrong," I interjected. "Human nature dictates that we perform and behave better when we're left to our own devices. There would be no lawlessness. We, the people, would ensure it."

The Governor continued to scour my list, grimacing visibly at a couple of points in his reading.

"I hate that goddamn metric system," he said. "That shit would never work over here. And diluting all of the alcohol would sure as hell take all of the fun out of hunting and fishing. No color television? Are you kidding? You can't watch a baseball game in black and white. It doesn't work. You can't tell which team is which and you can't see the baseball."

"Yes sir, there would certainly be an adjustment period but..."

"Hey! You mention Sammy Sosa here. He played for the Rangers! Still don't know what happened with that damn White Sox trade..."

"Well," I replied, "Harold Baines was a great professional hitter – didn't strike out much."

"Was Sosa part of the Baines deal? Or was that Alvarez?" the Governor asked, puzzled.

"I don't know, sir. I really don't remember."

Though he professed to like my ideas about shared bathrooms, homeowners associations and stench, it was clear that he had little or no intention of doing anything further with my proposal and he ended up dismissively waving me the hell away. Striking out with the Texas Governor was certainly a major blow and I knew then that things did not look good for my campaign to save the world. Despite the disappointment, I faxed my twelve steps to the United States President, the Queen of England and seven other major world leaders, pleading with them to allow me to save Mankind while I still could. In response, I received form letters from the leaders of Germany and France and a gold-plated medallion with a striped ribbon from the Queen of England. The United States President didn't respond to me directly but I think he mentioned me in a speech, referring to a "cook from Texas with bright eyes and little to stand up for".

My friends understood my intense commitment to these ideals and commiserated with me over my stinging failure. A rapper buddy who knew Coolio even offered to write and perform a charity rap song that would encompass and explain the twelve steps though, considering where his career was at the time, I figured that it would likely do more harm than good. For a while there, I rarely got out of bed and when I did, I certainly didn't bother to shower, shave or brush my teeth. My depression escorted me down a darkened road of despair until the day that a member of the group Herman's Hermits cornered me in an alley behind a Pacific Street deli.

"Snap out of it, bitch!" he screeched at what seemed like the top of his lungs.

"Bitch?" I was both scared and taken aback. "But I'm a dude, you know?"

"Quit feeling sorry for yourself, bitch, and give me something I can use. Don't want no half-baked freak show, now do I?"

"What are you talking about?" I asked, but the member of Herman's Hermits spun around and walked away muttering something about bacon, bridges and chives.

No, I didn't understand the words but the message was clear: Never ever quit on myself. And sometimes very good people can smell *very* bad.

#33

Downfall of a Perverted Friend

THE MOST SLIMY, BENEATH contempt yet loveable person I've ever known was this cat I met in Arlington named Rudolph, who preferred to be called Skyler or Sky. Skyler never held a real job in all of the years I knew him yet he always managed to collect monies through various shady dealings and assorted governmental agencies. He was what you might call a "chronic" womanizer who claimed to have bedded over 1700 women (and nineteen men) by the time he stopped keeping count due to dizziness from the inertia. The term "bedded" might be a bit misleading since the sex only sporadically occurred in actual beds; usually, his conquests took place in alleys, public restrooms, forests, cloves, vehicles of varying sizes, offices, parlors, laboratories, Eustace, airplanes, farms and deserted fireworks stands...even the apartments of cousins.

Skyler used the same pickup line for over twenty-five years and he used it on absolutely *every* woman he encountered. He would approach his subject and in his sexiest southern drawl say "You are, without doubt, the cutest thing known to man!" Skyler always preached the importance of doing whatever necessary to get the percentages into your favor, thus he would often tirelessly utilize his line on fifty or sixty women before getting a "hit" or what he called a "plench". Of course, in addition to a great line, he also possessed the advantage of being a decently attractive guy – over six feet tall, sandy blond hair, strong features, alabaster skin and pretty damn good hands, from what I could see. He used it all to his advantage and broke more than a few unfortunate hearts and other stuff along the way.

Skyler, in queer and contemptible fashion, never ever spoke to his conquests again after their initial encounter, however brief or substantive it might have been. With him, it was always and undoubtedly "one and done"; in fact, this became a creed of sorts to him and some of those who knew him. Skyler never had any desire for a long-term relationship; indeed, it was all about the thrill of the hunt and the eventual kill for him and he actually feared even the idea of any sort of lasting romance. He enjoyed living alone and wanted the women he screwed to be out of his life no later than ten minutes after his final orgasm of the session – and it was pretty much non-negotiable.

He was not at all particular in the types of women he targeted with his charms. Any woman (or feminine dude) was likely to be targeted if they toiled very long inside his self-proclaimed "circle of terror". Skyler picked up all sorts of women – small, huge and in between; homely, pretty and none of the above; young, old and in the middle. Much of it was semantics as far as he was concerned, and all that really mattered to him was scoring the ultimate victory in what he viewed as an ongoing war of the sexes. He would simply utter "You are, without doubt, the cutest thing known to man!" and then the battle of the genitals was joined with a vengeance.

The slimy side of Skyler usually emerged soon after his line had hooked either a willing participant or a sufficiently confused patient. He loved to make lewd, perverted suggestions concerning orifices, rope and ever-prevalent intangibles. He tended to use his damn good hands in ways that might make a very black registered nurse blush and always favored getting the physical action started immediately, regardless of the environment or privacy level. Thus, he became proficient in every kind of imaginable awkward position and also became accustomed to performing in front of peeping, grunting and hooting audiences of mainly men but sometimes an occasional lost woman here and there. Skyler was especially fond of the public restroom conquest but also seemed to have a soft spot for any location where dogs might be hanging around on the periphery.

Skyler's partners included women as old as eighty-one and girls as young as seventeen – despicable, no doubt. He had been with women that weighed over three hundred pounds and also some of the skinniest, sickliest human specimens imaginable. In his heyday, he "bedded" television stars, CEOs, politicians, naturalists, scientists, writers, military brass and inventors. At the same time, he was also "bedding" the homeless, drug addicts, pizza delivery girls, smokers, the handicapped, the mentally ill and girls from Michigan. Skyler was not at all discriminating when it came to his partners and simply commenced doing the deed with anyone who was agreeable to his proposition and in position to produce. I remember initially being somewhat envious of his lifestyle but I soon realized how sad and doomed his existence seemed to be. He literally had *no* other interests or passions in his life besides this bizarre game of chase and conquest.

One of Skyler's worst experiences resulting from his lifestyle was when he was accused of rape by a deluded marasmus patient. It was not a rape – the woman had been thrilled beyond words that Skyler was willing to penetrate her in the first place. But the accusation had caused him some problems with local law enforcement and also the media. Skyler was aghast when all of the local television news stations interviewed the shivering woman, who tearfully recounted her made-up charge. Not only was he indignant concerning her lies and exaggerations but he was embarrassed: The entire population of North Texas knew that he had physical relations with this hallucinating, plexor-toting wretch and his pride was wounded -- not enough to convince him to change his ways, mind you, but wounded nonetheless.

Another time that Skyler got himself into serious trouble was when he engaged in a quick sexual encounter with the married branch manager of a Department of Motor Vehicles office. He had taken notice of her when he was getting a drivers license renewal and she became positively giddy when he whispered his patented line into her clean and willing ear. So as to not arouse suspicion, she took Skyler out a side entrance of the building and straight into the backseat of a parked Texas State Troopers vehicle, which was apparently waiting with open arms though sirens were certainly not blaring. Skyler had, for some reason, been without sex for three days at that point and the resulting encounter only lasted a couple of minutes. The branch manager was somewhat chagrined by his performance but became totally enraged when he informed her that there would be no future relations or relationship. She produced a mini-machete that she had been somehow concealing in an armpit and attempted to perform a live castration; Skyler reacted immediately with a spontaneous lurch and the spurned woman's stabs only managed to remove about an eighth of an inch of basically unnecessary foreskin.

Though he emerged essentially intact, Skyler had bled for the rest of the day and was badly shaken for many months. He filed a formal complaint with the woman's district supervisor but no disciplinary action was ever administered and I'm pretty sure that she still works there to this day – at least that's what I've been told by someone nice.

Conquest #1761 and the event that finally scared him straight was drunken copulation with his best friend's wife in a men's restroom at Cowboys Stadium in Arlington. With the crowd cheering and phone cameras memorializing the action for posterity, Skyler thrust erratically and haphazardly, staggering around the restroom and dragging his best friend's wife around with him (since they were tentatively connected at the genitals). The two of them ended up tumbling to the urine-soaked floor in a heap and the encounter ended NOT with a Skyler climax but instead with a Skyler heart attack. The heart attack was a minor one but as he was being stretchered through the jovial, high-fiving crowd and out of the stadium, Skyler came to the conclusion that his life was seriously fucked up and he needed change in a major way. He made a solemn promise to himself then and there that he *would* change, that he *would* lead the kind of life that would make his parents and select descendants of Robert Rauschenberg very proud.

Thus, it was an incredibly ironic tragedy that while being treated at the hospital for the heart attack, it was discovered that Skyler was infested with at least twelve different venereal diseases of varying degrees of severity, including a previously unknown strain of syphilis that was ultimately named after him (Sky's Sandwiched Syphilis Spores). True, he probably should have noticed the discoloration, festering sores, rigid pubic twigs and syrup-textured urine. Still, Skyler was shattered when given the horrible news and was subsequently inconsolable – he really was. He spent the following seven days alternating between weeping, sleeping and swallowing illicit drugs covered in butterscotch and relish mixed with a quarter cup of Pine Sol.

Skyler felt lost, directionless and in need of a mint. He used his feces to sketch a map of the southeast quadrant of downtown Los Angeles on his bedroom wall and spent the better part of a day bottling his perspiration for the expressed purpose of resale. Skyler got a tattoo of a foot on his hand and situated his fireplace poker as an eyewitness to the resulting celebratory banquet. As Skyler began to believe that he might be losing his freaking mind, he reverted to the only behavior and lifestyle with which he was completely comfortable: He went to a local chewing gum dealership and told the cashier that "you are, without doubt, the cutest thing known to man". The flattery wowed the English-speaking foreign national and within three minutes, she was allowing Skyler full access to her somewhat-kempt private areas behind the checkout counter with security cameras whirring from their lofty perches. It didn't last long and Skyler left the gum store feeling disconsolate about his calculated and humiliating relapse.

Two or three days later, Skyler was arrested for passing a really bad check at a Home Depot and it was discovered that he had warrants… and warrants…and more warrants. His legal problems had, seemingly unbeknownst to him, mounted like the dickens throughout the previous few years and judge and jury condemned him to the Huntsville prison for a period of not less than eight years. It was obvious to all who knew him that Skyler would become quite deceased while imprisoned; he was too sick and his mind was too frail to enable him to deal with the day-to-day realities of such a horrid and unforgiving place.

Periodically, I would use my home computer or the one at the library on Center Street to look up relevant information on the incarcerated Skyler, just to check on his progress or lack thereof. I know for a fact that he lasted at least three years but I was never able to get any news on his behavior, state of mind or physical condition. After three years, it seemed that he simply vanished from the Texas prison system. I wasn't able to ascertain whether he died or if he had been released… or if something completely different had occurred such as an escape or inclusion into the cast of a low-end reality show.

I suppose it's conceivable that Skyler might still be alive in some isolated cove or fortified bunker in Central Texas. A friend of mine named Stanley told me that he was pretty sure he saw Skyler selling hotdogs and polish sausage from a portable cart at a flea market in Canton. A lady I used to like swears she saw him scooping manure on a spectator-lined parade route in downtown Atoka, Oklahoma. If he is out there somewhere, I find myself wondering if he wears a flag as a cape…or perhaps as a bonnet.

#34

An Incompetent Projectionist

BACK IN THE LATE nineties, I was constantly running into this eclectically dressed fellow named Hilton who was more of an acquaintance than he was a friend. He, however, seemed to view us as close friends and was continually talking up this film he was making that was supposed to change the world, or at least a couple of crucial sections of it. Every time I saw him, he insisted on updating me about the film's progress and made me promise to attend the lavish premier he was busily planning. The title of the film had been adjusted a few times during production but he had finally settled on "A Visit to Hell...Ribbed For Her Pleasure".

The premise of the film was that it was based on a real-life near-death experience that had been haunting Hilton since a drug overdose when he was twenty-five years old. He had clinically died according to the emergency room doctors at Parkland and Hilton always claimed that he actually went to Hell during the ordeal and though he was only gone for a few minutes at the hospital, he said that his time in Hell seemed like it lasted a year or more. Hilton's movie was to be a re-creation of his experience while toiling in the Devil's domain and he was anxious to share it with the entire world plus all unshaven auto detailers.

Hilton shot his film utilizing a series of hand-held camcorders in addition to strategically placed still photo frames. His attempt to hire big-name Hollywood actors had essentially failed; he was never able to get through to Sylvester Stallone or Keanu Reeves, who were his top choices to play his role. Hilton was able to reach Gilbert Gottifred, who kept putting him off and would never offer any kind of firm or steady commitment. He settled on a local stage actor from Denton named Cesar who had movie star good looks except for a missing ear from a childhood fireworks accident and really, really terrible acne. He filled out the rest of the cast with patrons from a Denny's, a Bedford-based drug store pharmacist, assorted street urchins, nine high school delinquents and David Lee Roth.

When the day of the big premier came, I arrived at the rented theatre with pretty damn low expectations. It simply did not appear to me that Hilton was operating with a "full deck" and from the details I had heard, it didn't seem that he had hit on any real formula for success in this moviemaking venture. I was actually surprised when I got there because there were probably two hundred people milling about in the lobby, including many of the Dallas beautiful and elite whom I was accustomed to seeing on television and in the gossip section of the area newspapers. The biggest radio personality in town was strolling around with his two hands crammed down the front of his pants and a maniacal grin on his chummy face. Dallas' top plastic surgeon was bitching because the concession stand was closed and demanded that it be opened so that he could get a hotdog with mustard and a look from a schoolgirl. The Wilson brothers were tossing a football around as Henley looked on, forlorn and even a bit reproached. An actress – whose face I knew but name I did not – was breastfeeding a stranger's baby, both as a favor and because, as she kept repeating, it was "so damn much fun".

"The theatre is now open…please come in and find yourself a seat," announced a dangerously overweight black man wearing what looked to be a custom-made bellhop's uniform in a combination of navy blue and turquoise plaid.

Former NFL player Coy Bacon sprinted to be the first through the theater doors, followed by the brother of Cubby from the original Mousketeers and the remainder of the shuffling, murmuring crowd. I was one of the last people to enter the chilly, darkened room and found a seat on the aisle in the very back row with Markie Mark two seats over but nobody in the seat beside me. In the minutes after everyone was seated, what had been a murmur became a dull, impatient roar as people began to wonder aloud what they were in for, until the moment Hilton stepped to the front of the theater and held his hands up for silence.

"Ladies and Gentlemen – you're in for a real treat – a *real* treat. I am about to screen for you my life's work – my *life's* work. I have never been so excited about anything in all my years and I am thrilled to have all of you here to share it with me. It's a movie, you know, but it's so much more than that; it's art, it's life, it's death, it's love, it's allegory and it's hate. You will be moved to tears and you'll laugh hysterically. In the next hour, you will feel every range of emotion known to man, you know, and you will leave here a changed person – changed for the better, I hope. This may well be the most crucial and important hour of your life, you know, and I think you'll agree with me that my masterpiece is a potent and powerful piece of work. You were each selected to be here because of your special individual relationship with me and I feel so privileged that you took the time out of your busy schedules to come out this evening. I guarantee that you will be glad you did. And so, without further ado..."

Hilton made a grand finger gesture toward the little projector room above our heads in the back of the theatre and the movie began to roll. The opening scene, which was shaking a bit due to the instability of hand-held cameras, took place in what appeared to be an Old West saloon or tavern. There was festive piano music being played with maybe a few horns tossed in for good measure as grimy cowboys and eccentric saloon girls danced around drunkenly in their dusty, grubby garb. At a wooden table in the middle of the place, a card game had been interrupted by the desire of the participants to begin snorting coke from the back of each other's hands. It was a pretty funny sight to see tough looking cowboys with their cowboy hats and gun belts sniffing the sensational powder from the backs of their fellow player's dirty hands. All at once, Cesar from Denton made his first appearance as a slope-shouldered ocean biologist wearing cardigan and chanting Hare Krishna in a woman's voice.

The scene switched immediately to a Parisian meat market with irreparable breaches in the roof and a full-sized tugboat sitting weirdly in the middle of the place. The gay meat shoppers maneuvered deftly around the tugboat to make their selections from the freezers and coolers that lined the walls and they carefully stacked their packages into supermarket-style shopping carts and, in some cases, onto the tops of their own heads. Many of the establishment's patrons were morbidly obese and likely suffered from violently enlarged prostates, based on their contorted faces and the sheer number of trips to the meat market's bathroom. Cesar was in the middle of it all using a turn-of-the-century pricing gun to affix price stickers to the meat and it was as if everything in the place cost only a U.S. penny and a smile.

When the meat market sold out of its meat, the film transported us to a secure research department in West Memphis that was dedicated to the discovery of a cure for lactose intolerance. The scientists therein were consequently naked and communicated through a coordinated series of clicks, snaps and tongue gymnastics. The male scientists had colorfully painted toenails and the female scientists had hairy "man asses" with crazy "ass dimples" and permanent bug tattoos made from real authentic bug matter. The cure for lactose intolerance proved to be elusive and the scientists contented themselves with discovering a cure for anteaters that only cost a couple a bucks, if that.

Then Cesar from Denton appeared on-screen dressed as a Haitian mapmaker holding up a hand-painted placard with the words "Hell is not and cannot be extracted from your mane". The screen plunged into a temporary blackness that took your breath away before lighting up again in the midst of a manger scene with David Lee Roth in the place of the baby Jesus. A fire ignited from David Lee Roth's testicles and soon everything – manger, farm animals, straw, wise men, David Lee Roth – was dangerously ablaze. The fire roared out of control and what was cool was that Hilton had somehow managed to import the aroma of burning flesh into the theatre, which was a neat and surprising little trick. I'm guessing the fire burned on for a good ten minutes before ending with a thud and leaving nothing but a solemn Cesar on screen, staring emotionlessly at the audience with a badly burned dove carcass cradled in his hands. His gaze was professional, if a bit mechanical, and when he pursed his lips and licked his teeth in anticipation of speaking, I noticed an audible gasp amongst those in the crowd around me.

"Hell is real and if you think I'm lying, you're a fucker. Hell is only a few minutes away and when you look past your own conceit, you can plainly see the royal blue street sign ringed in fire. It's a troubling place devoid of any notable pleasure or circumstance and lacking in creature comforts to beat the band. I went to Hell once but the Devil didn't latch on securely enough and I'm back here to warn you all that you need to change your drugging, whoring and evil ways. If you don't, you will end up in Hell and I frankly don't think many of you could handle it all that well. Hell is NOT the place to be – it really isn't and you need to take my word for that."

With that, the hand-held camera panned slowly but surely away from Cesar's acne-scarred face and across a blank solid white wall, moving stealthily around the sparse room until it settled onto a small, sturdy end table made of some kind of weird oak. On the table lay a single, long-stemmed red rose that was beginning to curl and blacken around the edges from some kind of sickness or disorder. The camera focused its gaze on the rose for an uncomfortably extended period of time before the scene faded literally to black. Then, in florescent green splendor, the words "Hilton loves ya baby...and you know it has to be true!" appeared and it was as if each of the letters was doing some kind of little dance or jig. After a couple of minutes of this, the film's credits started to roll and the lights in theatre began to gradually illuminate.

A bit of an awkward pause ensued before former Cowboys quarterback Gary Hogeboom stood and began a slow, reverential hand clapping. He was joined by Pat Boone and baby Jessica and soon the entire audience was on its feet showering applause and whoops onto the smiling, blushing and seemingly expanding Hilton. It was certainly his proudest moment and he reveled in the waves of adulation that washed down upon him from the adoring crowd and managed to stifle his need to belch aloud for the duration of the ovation.

I remember feeling profound sadness when word came down from the projection room that the projectionist had unintentionally ruined Hilton's masterpiece with a combination of rum, bean dip and dull safety scissors. And I also remember my sadness being compounded when it was discovered that Hilton had neglected to make any copies of his film – the destroyed copy was the *only* copy. Thus, I felt only sympathy for Hilton when he told us all to "rot in Hell" and began marching around the place like an emboldened Nazi soldier on crack or possibly something even worse than crack.

Epilogue

I KNEW THIS GUY a long time ago that appeared to have the actual face of a field mouse – a giant goddamn field mouse face – and despite his unfortunate and queer affliction he had the absolute coolest outlook on life. I don't even remember his name but he steadfastly maintained that true happiness had nothing at all to do with accumulated wealth, frequent and intense ejaculations or God-given talent and looks. According to my friend with the field mouse face, the keys to a truly happy and fulfilling life were simple: Consumption of three semi-rotten jalapeno peppers every single day; encircling yourself with loved ones but being careful not to see them too often; and hiring a dependable lawn service to perform all necessary lawn and garden actions.

To me, I've always felt that the best way to achieve pure happiness is to avoid pain at all costs. Sometimes, no matter how hard you attempt to avoid it, pain will come a' calling. When it does, I have always felt it crucial to possess a more than sufficient supply of potent "pain-numbing" materials to deal with the crisis. For physical torment, great strides have been made in the development of increasingly more effective over-the-counter medications and ointments. Ginger ale mixed with warm and cloudy cognac produces a terrific pain fighting substance that will also occasionally serve as a sympathetic liquid shoulder to cry on. I've never really liked doctors but many of them are proficient and generous in the writing of prescriptions; when receiving an ample prescription for pain medication, it is imperative that you strive to save as much as possible for a "rainy day". I learned this the hard way and can assure you that you will always be glad you did.

Mental, emotional and spiritual pain can be tricky to avoid but it is important to do so – at least, as much as humanly possible. Denial can be a great defense mechanism, as can literally turning the other damn cheek. When my feelings get hurt or when someone insults me verbally, I like to look the offender direct in the eyes and ask, "do you eat Paulus Potter with that mouth?" which usually results in a stammered, uncertain answer that I might find humorous or I might find as puzzling as live game hen. There are people out there that absolutely delight in mentally abusing others that they deem weak or inferior; these are what I like to call "mental bullies" and there really ought to be a stern law against them, though there currently isn't in my state.

Besides kidney stones, the worst agony I have endured in my life is when I have loved someone that did not love me. It happened to me a few times in my younger days and each time was an excruciatingly painful ordeal that left me beaten, drained and in dire need of professional therapy or something akin. Unfortunately for me, I bypassed the therapy and dealt with the rejection in unhealthy ways that made me vulnerable to the predatory nature of opportunists and night stalkers. Certainly, love can be a gift from the heavens above but it can just as certainly be a self-righteous poison pill that induces chills, convulsions, fever, vomiting through the mouth *and* nose, in addition to challenging urination. Those fortunate folks who have been lucky in love are the luckiest people on Earth – they really are. Me? Things eventually turned out well but the road to that point was fraught with nicks, cuts and slashes that frequently drove me to my goddamn surgically repaired knees.

I'm reasonably sure it was Ralph J. Bunche or Herm Edwards who once uttered, "Love feels like a meatless picnic during a hailstorm for the ages." The comment – both astute and bizarre – has caused me to reassess a certain position or situation on numerous occasions through the years and has also enabled me to reflect without regret. These days, my emotional well-being stands tall and straight and, thus, I've been able to maintain a proportionately centered existence. Things haven't gone perfectly – far from it – but I've managed to learn the appropriate lessons and hid away in a nearby drafty broom closet when the situation dictated.

I've long been acquainted with these two journeyman rappers called Master Pilla and Bizzy B, who both curiously outgrew their pants at a staid high school coronation of sorts. For reasons known only to them, they determined that their best solution was to learn a foreign language and, after careful consideration, they chose German. Once they became proficient in German, they never wore pants again. I've always admired their fortitude; these two young people – and their general nakedness – are on my mind nearly every single day, along with other items such as bills, stars, forcible entry, root beer, snot and not-so-bloody razors.

In the end, the pain you can see is infinitely more tolerable than the pain you cannot. When the issue of pain is scrutinized intensely, it becomes crystal clear that the solution you seek is all in the math. Hopefully, it adds up. And if it doesn't? Close the window, turn up the heat and toss the dice like you mean it…like you really mean it.